T0251549

Collection Development in a Digital Environment

Sul H. Lee
Editor

Collection Development in a Digital Environment has been co-published simultaneously as *Journal of Library Administration,* Volume 28, Number 1 1999.

CRC Press
Taylor & Francis Group
Boca Raton   London   New York

CRC Press is an imprint of the
Taylor & Francis Group, an informa business

Collection Development in a Digital Environment has been co-published simultaneously as *Journal of Library Administration,* Volume 28, Number 1 1999.

The development, preparation, and publication of this work has been undertaken with great care. However, the publisher, employees, editors, and agents of The Haworth Press and all imprints of The Haworth Press, Inc., including The Haworth Medical Press® and Pharmaceutical Products Press®, are not responsible for any errors contained herein or for consequences that may ensue from use of materials or information contained in this work. Opinions expressed by the author(s) are not necessarily those of The Haworth Press, Inc.

Library of Congress Cataloging-in-Publication Data

University of Oklahoma. Libraries. Conference (1998)
    Collection development in a digital environment / Sul H. Lee, editor.
      p. cm.
    A series of papers presented at the 1998 University of Oklahoma Libraries Conference: "Challenges of collection development : digital information, Internet, and print materials"–Introd.
    "Co-published simultaneously as Journal of library administration', Vol. 28, no. 1, 1999."
    Includes bibliographical references and index.
    ISBN 0-7890-0794-0 (alk. paper). – ISBN 0-7890-0827-0
    1. Academic libraries–Collection development–United States Congresses. 2. Libraries–United States–Special collections–Electronic information resources Congresses. I. Lee, Sul H. II. Title. III. Title: Journal of library administration, vol. 28. No. 1.
    Z675.U5U575 1998
    025.2'187'0973–dc21   99-39118
                                                                        CIP

ABOUT THE EDITOR

Sul H. Lee, Dean of the University Libraries, University of Oklahoma, is an internationally recognized leader and consultant in the library administration and management field. Dean Lee is a past member of the Board of Directors, Association of Research Libraries, the ARL Office of Management Services Advisory Committee, and the Council for the American Library Association. His works include *The Impact of Rising Costs of Serials and Monographs on Library Services and Programs*; *Library Material Costs and Access to Information*; *Budgets for Acquisitions: Strategies for Serials, Monographs, and Electronic Formats*; *Vendor Evaluation and Acquisition Budgets*; *Collection Assessment and Acquisitions Budgets*; *The Role and Future of Special Collections in Research Libraries*; *Declining Acquisitions Budgets*; and *Access, Ownership, and Resource Sharing*. He is also Editor of *Journal of Library Administration*.

Collection Development in a Digital Environment

CONTENTS

Introduction

One of the joys of developing an annual conference at the University of Oklahoma is the opportunity to work with some of the outstanding thinkers in our profession. This volume contains a series of thought-provoking papers presented at the 1998 University of Oklahoma Libraries Conference, "Challenges of Collection Development: Digital Information, Internet and Print Materials." You will recognize many of the presenters as leaders in our profession and I appreciate their thoughtful papers, which stimulated fascinating discussions throughout the conference. While this publication does not record those discussions, I am pleased to introduce this set of articles to you with the hope it will stimulate you to think about and further discuss these important issues related to collection development.

James Neal, Director of the Milton S. Eisenhower Library at Johns Hopkins University, points to revolutionary changes in the profession and advocates libraries taking the lead in advancing the academic agenda through technology, while at the same time recognizing technology requires change in libraries. Milton Wolf, Vice President for Collection Development Programs at the Center for Research Libraries, continues the idea of change in libraries and promotes the need to collaborate in this new environment.

Kenneth Frazier, Director, General Library Systems at the University of Wisconsin, discusses the ethical dilemmas of library collection development and offers some suggestions on how libraries may meet these dilemmas. He suggests the idea of "disintermediation" in the publishing process. Dennis Dillon, Head, Collection and Information Resources at the University of Texas at Austin, questions and examines the influence of the World Wide Web on the role of librarians. He also raises the idea of "disintermediation."

[Haworth co-indexing entry note]: "Introduction." Lee, Sul H. Co-published simultaneously in *Journal of Library Administration* (The Haworth Information Press, an imprint of The Haworth Press, Inc.) Vol. 28, No. 1, 1999, pp. 1-2; and: *Collection Development in a Digital Environment* (ed: Sul H. Lee) The Haworth Information Press, an imprint of The Haworth Press, Inc., 1999, pp. 1-2. Single or multiple copies of this article are available for a fee from The Haworth Document Delivery Service [1-800-342-9678, 9:00 a.m. - 5:00 p.m. (EST). E-mail address: getinfo@haworthpressinc.com].

Mary Case, Director of the Office of Scholarly Communications at the Association of Research Libraries, and Deborah Jakubs, Director of Collection Services at Duke University, describe the importance of international resources in today's environment. While international emphasis is increasing, libraries' acquisition of expanding international publishing is declining. Their paper describes some initiatives by the Association of Research Libraries to improve global access to information.

Joan Giesecke, Dean, University Libraries at the University of Nebraska, presents the reader with an interesting discussion on "scenario driven planning" and describes its use in collection development planning.

The final two papers focus on the roles of vendors in the electronic environment. Kathleen Born, Vice President and Director, academic Division of EBSCO Information Services, discusses a new role for subscription agents as "aggregators." She probes the working relationship with publishers and describes models developed by vendors for electronic delivery. Kit Kennedy, Director of Academic Sales for Blackwell's Information Services, considers the activities of librarians and suggests a new role for the vendor as "Information Coach."

The value of any conference is a combination of quality presentations and interested participants. The University of Oklahoma Libraries Conference has been fortunate to bring together a wonderful mix of people to investigate important issues of the day. I look forward to continuing these presentations and publishing the papers in the future.

I would like to thank Don Hudson for his work as Conference Coordinator. His organization skills are greatly appreciated. I would also like to thank Melanie Davidson and Wilbur Stolt for their work in producing this volume.

Sul H. Lee, Dean
University of Oklahoma Libraries

Chaos Breeds Life:
Finding Opportunities
for Library Advancement
During a Period
of Collection Schizophrenia

James G. Neal

Academic libraries are being transformed by powerful forces and fundamental changes in global learning, information technology and scholarly communication. To remain vital to the university's learning and research excellence, libraries must also become agents of transformation, participating in the reshaping of the higher education enterprise. This will require a revisioning of the library's future development and a fundamental rethinking of the economic models which underpin and define library growth and success.

The academic library's survival, and its relevance and centrality to the mission of the university, is dependent on a new vision of advancement. The future library must pursue strategic thinking, fiscal agility and entrepreneurial approaches to the development of collections and services, and to the expansion of its markets. The processes of information acquisition, organization, navigation and archiving, the activities that libraries have carried out for centuries, must be focused in-

---

James G. Neal is Director of the Milton S. Eisenhower Library, Johns Hopkins University.

[Haworth co-indexing entry note]: "Chaos Breeds Life: Finding Opportunities for Library Advancement During a Period of Collection Schizophrenia." Neal, James G. Co-published simultaneously in *Journal of Library Administration* (The Haworth Information Press, an imprint of The Haworth Press, Inc.) Vol. 28, No. 1, 1999, pp. 3-17; and: *Collection Development in a Digital Environment* (ed: Sul H. Lee) The Haworth Information Press, an imprint of The Haworth Press, Inc., 1999, pp. 3-17. Single or multiple copies of this article are available for a fee from The Haworth Document Delivery Service [1-800-342-9678, 9:00 a.m. - 5:00 p.m. (EST). E-mail address: getinfo@haworthpressinc.com].

3

creasingly on customized and interactive access to integrated multimedia at point of need. It must also incorporate innovative applications of technology and artificial intelligence systems. The model of the global digital library views the organization as both a provider of global publications and as a gateway for users to digital resources around the world, as both an historical archive and as a research and learning collaboratory. The academic library, particularly in its program of collection development and information access, must behave almost chameleon-like over at least the next decade as the current schizophrenic information environment is transformed. As Yogi Berra once said: "When you come to a fork in the road, take it."

David Close, in his book *The Meaning of Revolution*, emphasizes that "the essential feel of revolution derives from its cataclysmic quality . . . it destroys people's security and unsettles their convictions." Thomas Kuhn, in *The Structure of Scientific Revolutions*, notes that "the transition from a paradigm in crisis to a new one from which a new tradition can emerge is far from a cumulative process." Karl Marx, in his theory of knowledge, points to quantitative change leading to qualitative change, the transformation which he calls revolution. Academic libraries are confronted by a series of revolutionary changes which are shaping collection development programs in dramatic ways:

- The personal computing revolution is at the core of individualized technology and the expanding power to access, communicate, analyze and control information.
- The electronic revolution is producing vast amounts of digital information in all media and intelligent software that enables effective search and retrieval.
- The network revolution is creating a vast telecommunications web and critical platforms for a renaissance in such areas as personal communication, publishing, distributed learning and commercial development.
- The cellular revolution is enabling an expanding sense of freedom from place, of being able to communicate and access information whenever and wherever.
- The music television/video games revolution is cultivating a generation of new learners and consumers who demand a more graphical, integrated, and interactive multimedia presentation of information.

- The robotics revolution is advancing programmed mechanical tools and intelligent agents to take on routine and repetitive processes.
- The virtual reality revolution is enabling a variety of computer-generated experiences and simulations with broad applications in entertainment, education and work settings.
- The security/encryption revolution presents a pressing information access challenge, as we seek to implement authentication tools for enabling appropriate uses of information and to protect privacy and the security of network communication.
- The hypertext revolution is building robust and powerful links among millions of networked files and enabling navigation among the rich intricacies of the integrated if still chaotic Internet.
- The push revolution is shifting the nature of Web searching by narrowcasting to network users through customized packaging and delivery of information.
- The privatization or outsourcing revolution is moving basic operations out of the organization to external providers.
- The self-service or ATM revolution is encouraging a fundamental rethinking of user services in an environment where user-initiated and user-controlled activities are now commonplace.
- The partnership revolution is producing higher levels of cooperation and collaboration among organizations as a fundamental requirement for success and as a tool for resource sharing.
- The authorship revolution is defining the facility and the creativity potential of the Web where, with a minimal investment, one can post information to numerous potential readers on a global scale.
- The entrepreneurial revolution is encouraging creators and distributors of networked information to explore the commercial potential of the Internet and the new market niches being created for products and services.
- The business concentration revolution is highlighting the global business linkages developing in many industries and the economic, political and social impacts of monopolistic practices.
- The new majority student revolution is bringing into the academic community waves of individuals who have not traditionally attended college and whose family, job and personal responsibilities demand very innovative responses from higher education.

- The values revolution is pointing to the growing political and social schisms under the impact of technology change and the expanding threats to intellectual freedom, privacy, and the free flow of information.
- The intellectual property revolution is threatening fair use rights for digital information and creating conflicts between the interests of information providers and information consumers.
- The government information revolution is transforming the creation, distribution and use of publications and data from the nation's and world's largest publishing sources, as they become increasingly electronic and network-based.
- The digital preservation revolution is energizing us to be concerned about the integrity and archiving for future use of the vast amount of electronic information being produced and lost.
- The information as commodity revolution is increasingly viewing data and its synthesized products, knowledge, as articles of commerce and sources of profit rather than property held in common for societal good.
- The global awareness revolution is supporting the internationalization of all aspects of life and encouraging a new world view of networked collections and services.
- The knowledge management revolution is spawning a new relationship among researcher, librarian and information technologist which maximizes the usefulness of data gathering, information generation and distribution.
- The virtuality revolution is energizing all organizations to think and plan beyond the envelope of place-based capabilities and to create innovative approaches to the design and delivery of new products and services to expanding markets.

These twenty-five trends only begin to describe the dynamic environment in which academic libraries are developing. They support the evolving models of future library development. The "virtual library" evolves as "a seamless web of interconnected, coordinated and interdependent collections that are accessible to geographically distributed users." We can talk about this new paradigm because of the confluence of powerful desktop workstations, sophisticated user software, the ubiquitous network, expanding electronic publishing, and extraordinary user expectations.

But the model of virtuality is not achievable unless we also accept the importance of the virtuoso library and its ability to manage the volume, cost and diversity of scholarly information and to bring together substantive subject, language, technical and professional skills in the areas of selection, acquisition, organization, service, education, access and preservation. This model also demands the virtuous library, that is a library willing and able to share collections, technology and expertise; to work in partnership with academic units, publishers, government agencies, and corporations; and to influence national information policy and advocate aggressively for users. It is no longer viable just to buy materials for the collections just in case our faculty and students may need them at some point. We must develop a capability to move beyond anticipation to responsiveness and customization, where "just in time" and "just for you" become the standards of information access.

A number of definitions have been advanced to describe "the digital library." The University of California posits the digital library as "a set of human, financial, and technological systems which enable knowledge generation, access and use with four primary roles: information preservation, storage and retrieval; electronic access and delivery via electronic communications; online publishing of the scholarly and scientific knowledge base; and information management consultation and training." The Digital Library Federation has advanced a different focus: "Digital libraries are organizations that provide the resources, including the specialized staff to select, organize, provide intellectual access to, interpret, distribute, preserve the integrity of, and ensure the persistence over time of collections of digital works so that they are readily and economically available for use by a defined community or set of communities." The DLF has advanced four programmatic priorities: a focus on libraries of born materials and less on conversion of analog resources; the integration of digital materials into academic and community life; the development of the core digital library infrastructure; and the provision of organizational support for the effective management of digital libraries.

The institutional digital library program should include several core elements, including scholarly content, instructional support, technology development, access design, and research and evaluation. Its collection and service content should focus on the following components:

- the purchase and licensing from commercial sources of electronic publications and databases
- the development and acquisition of a next-generation library management system with graphical user interface and Web capabilities
- the identification and organization of access to Web materials of quality and relevance
- the conversion of analog materials to digital formats
- the provision of electronic course reserves/digital classroom
- the collection and archiving of software, courseware, simulations and research datafiles
- on-demand direct delivery to users of articles and research papers
- customized literature update services
- the management of institutional records and archives
- the design of online instructional tutorials to support effective use of networked resources
- the provision of online reference services, including artificial intelligence systems

At the core of these developments is a technological infrastructure which is robust and reliable, and which is characterized by sufficient connectivity and capacity and quality performance. Libraries must be in a leadership position to advance the academic agenda through technology:

- universal access to integrated information, including computation and productivity on the desktop workstation, high-performance shared computer resources, high-speed access to scholarly and institutional information, and the ability to find and filter information
- support for access and use of information, including digital network development and management, instructional computing and multimedia deliverable to campus classrooms and other learning sites, research and scientific computing support, and the application of information technology to the administrative work of the university
- the creation and distribution of digital information
- tools for analyzing and manipulating information
- collaboration and leadership in information technology research and in the area of information policy

This agenda requires that libraries advance from using technology for replication and acceleration, that is doing the things we have always done but much faster, to using technology to innovate, to do new things, and to advance the transformation of learning and scholarship. Our experience with technology has identified those critical conditions which improve the positive impact:

- if the technology is more ubiquitous so that it is directly available to the user, and the user has a sense of control
- if more developed technology capacity is available
- if users have greater competency and experience with the technology
- if the technology experts are more responsive to the felt needs of the user regarding the design of the system
- if users routinely rather than selectively use technology and information systems

Users bring significant expectations to technology, including more and better content, access and convenience, new capabilities, cost reduction, and organizational and individual productivity. Technology development should be user-centered, focused from the outset on the needs of the user and enabling users to participate as members of the design team in experimental and iterative design.

As we build the digital library, it is critical that we both understand and maximize the important advantages of the digital medium:

- accessibility, to overcome the limitations of place
- availability, to dispense with the limitations of time
- searchability, to probe works in new ways
- currency, to make information available more timely
- researchability, to ask new questions that could not be posed with a printed text
- dynamism, the fluidity of the presentation and the ability to re-shape the information
- interdisciplinarity, to carry out inquiries across multiple fields and to explore new approaches to a topic
- collaborative nature, to incorporate conversation and debate into the use and development of a work
- multimedia aspects, to integrate text, images, sound and video

- linkability, to use hypertext capabilities to connect to related materials around the world
- interactivity, to not only read and view the information, but also to manipulate the text and images
- procedural qualities, the ability of the computer to carry out tasks over and over again with high accuracy and efficiency, thus allowing the user to focus on the intellectual work
- encyclopedic potential, that is the almost unlimited capacity of the computer to store and display massive volumes of information without the restrictions of the physical format

But we must not overlook the important advantages of the printed text: its portability, durability, readability, markupability, archivability, ownability, affordability, familiarity, and aesthetic qualities. We must also understand the importance of an individual's relationship to the medium:

- physicality, the tangibility of the book, and the difference between turning a page and clicking a mouse
- geography, the orientation of the reader to the text and the differences in the ability to see where one has been and where one is going
- psychology, the variation of the nature and results of the experience when reading and handling a recent paperback edition of a text versus a sixteenth century illustrated folio volume of the work, a difference lost online
- sociology, the isolation of computer use versus the multiple possibilities of reading experiences from a book, such as out loud and group experiences
- cognition, the linear nature of the book versus the hypertext and interactive online process, and a single work in book form versus an online collection

Electronic publishing has provoked a far more complex process for making information available in electronic formats. The steps and considerations involved are very different from print acquisition, and include: awareness of the material, evaluation for purchase often more rigorous because of price, consultation with prospective users, selection, exploration of consortial purchase, financing, negotiation with publisher, ordering from publisher, negotiating license agreement, establishing technical platform, creating user access and presentation, implementing the hardware, implementing the required software, creating bibliographic record, making users aware of availability and educating in effective use, assessing the level and quality of use, evaluating the impact on print collections, arranging for appropriate updating, and making provision for archiving of the information.

Similarly, the networked information environment has produced an array of licensing or purchase options which determine what a library pays for user access, and these include: subscription site license, a transaction or per use charge, volume or consortial discounts, payment for value-added features, simultaneous user access systems, purchase and ownership of the information, price reductions through sponsored subsidies, and free access through development partnerships. These acquisition models have contributed to a very complex information marketplace.

Digital library programs require new staff expertise. In the Eisenhower Library at Johns Hopkins, the following positions have been created and filled over the past year: digital knowledge center director, digital production specialist, digital multimedia specialist, graduate student digital project assistants, digital archiving specialist, electronic resource center manager, Web development coordinator, Web design specialist, electronic and distance learning specialist, microcomputer/ software training specialist, network support staff, electronic resources coordinator, Unix specialist staff, metadata/digital cataloging specialist, digital database/server support staff, library management system coordinator, electronic reference specialist, information/network literacy specialist, fine arts/digital images specialist, electronic exhibits coordinator, electronic course reserves coordinator and foundation/corporate funding coordinator.

There is also a need for new physical spaces, and at Hopkins' Eisenhower Library, the following have been implemented over the past year: an electronic resource center, which serves as a reference and teaching facility; the digital knowledge center and its laboratory and consultation areas; the digital photography lab; wired reader accommodations across the building to provide network access for portable computers; systems help desk; digital copying and delivery center; server equipment rooms with appropriate environmental conditions; electronic reserves production center; digital government information and GIS center; and electronic exhibit center.

Similarly, the organization of the library has to evolve and new units have to be created. Such a unit in the Eisenhower Library is the new Digital Knowledge Center. It serves as a campus hub for the creation, production, marketing, distribution and archiving of electronic multimedia information and instructional resources. It is a laboratory for experimenting with and employing new technologies in teaching, learning and scholarship. Its areas of activities include: electronic publishing and new forums for faculty research, emerging technologies, electronic course development and multimedia digital kits, online exhibits, intellectual property management, and digital library projects.

The redefinition of our physical infrastructure, our staff expertise and our organizational framework must be complemented by an external involvement for the library in the national and international information policy arenas. Libraries are confronting the copyright challenge which is threatening fair use exemptions for digital information and creating extraordinary conflict between the interests of information providers and information consumers. Whether it's the battery of legislation being considered in Congress this year, the international treaties shaped at WIPO in Geneva which may be unfriendly to American legal traditions and academic values, the licensing agreements we sign at our libraries which too frequently give away rights, the pressure for the creation of use guidelines which threaten to establish prematurely inappropriate and unnecessary rules of behavior, the debates in the academy on the ownership of intellectual property, and the technological solutions in the form of copyright management systems, these six streams of copyright activity threaten the fundamental and constitutionally protected balance which is essential to teaching, research and the work of libraries.

There are other information policy areas that command the attention of the academic library as we build digital collections, and these include free speech and inquiry, privacy, telecommunications regulation and universal service. The development of the national telecommunications infrastructure through the work of the research universities' Internet-2 imitative and the government's next-generation Internet plan is critical to library success. The Internet-2 movement seeks to recreate and sustain a leading-edge network capability for the learning and research communities, to refocus network development on a new generation of applications that fully exploit the potential of broadband networks, and to coordinate national development with campus and community production networks.

Our collections are central to the radical expansion of the higher education learning environment and the ability to take the educational experience, including the academic support services like the library, out of the campus classroom to the student. It also speaks to the enhancement of the classroom learning experience through the creative application of network technologies and electronic content. Think about the new education markets being pursued by our institutions and how the library can be a core player in enabling this critical expansion of education beyond the traditional resident student:

- facilitating employment transitions and career changes for adult learners
- liberal arts colleges preparing perpetual learners who will be seeking intellectual growth and challenge throughout their lives
- graduate education as a gateway to continuous collaboration and global scholarship
- daily learning sustaining teams of knowledge workers in the world's factories, offices and laboratories
- network scholarship beginning before college as universities expand into the K-12 community

Each of these thrusts will demand new thinking about how to deliver information resources and collaborative tools to distributed students.

The digital library will also be a critical tool for transforming the processes of scholarly communication. Scholarly activity is the creation of new knowledge and the evaluation of its validity, the preservation of information and its transmission to others. The community of production, traditionally the authors and publishers, and the community of consumption, that is libraries and readers, are becoming blurred under the impact of shifting technologies, economics and roles. Scholarship is routinely circulating on the global network, and the academic library will be a central player in refining the information value chain. The functions performed across this chain: information generation and creation, authoring, informal peer communication, editorial work and validation, definition of ownership, distribution, acquisition and access, storage, preservation and archiving, information management, location and delivery, recognition, diffusion and utilization, all are being reshaped.

The current academic publishing model is in crisis. The world production of new information continues to explode. The cost of research publications continues to inflate at unprecedented rates. Acquisitions budgets have not kept pace with inflation, particularly for journals in science, engineering and medicine. The more expensive commercial publishers are taking over from academic and society publishers and there is a troubling consolidation taking place in the publishing industry. There has been a very significant decline in the purchase of new scholarly monographs by research libraries and the buying public. The electronic production, storage and distribution of research information is of growing importance in many disciplines. The publication of new scholarly information in the form of new journals and books increases every year. The cumulative impact of these trends has been aggressively documented by the Association of Research Libraries.

We must understand the urge to publish as we respond to these conditions, why the faculty on our campuses are so highly motivated to share their research results with colleagues. Clearly, scholars want to communicate their research and they are concerned with the preservation of their ideas. They have been nurtured in an academic culture which celebrates scholarship and which links prestige, recognition and rewards to productivity and scholarly output, And for some there is even profit from publishing activity. These motivations must be recognized as we implement new models of electronic scholarly publishing.

One can argue that the best way to predict the future is to invent it. In that spirit, last year Johns Hopkins hosted a meeting of university presidents, provosts, librarians, publishers and researchers under the aegis of the Pew Higher Education Roundtable to discuss this crisis in scholarly communication. Several key issues were identified:

- the imbalance in information price relative to value and source costs
- the time lag between authorship, peer review, publication and dissemination
- the imbalance in information authorship, ownership and proprietary rights
- the under-recognition of these conditions as an important public policy issue

There was also understanding of how institutions have been managing the situation through: journal cancellations and reduced acquisitions, improved document delivery services to users, cooperative collection development activities, site licensing for electronic information resources, and consortial purchases by groups of institutions. Several important conclusions were reached. What has been discussed for decades as the library problem must now be embraced as a concern of the entire university community. We must move away from the gift exchange society that we have created, the corporate economy that has taken over what was a guild economy, which encourages faculty researchers to give their work to publishers only to have the libraries on their campuses buy it back at ever increasing prices. This is particularly problematic when so much of this research is being funded with public dollars through federal grants. We are choking on the proliferation of publication and thus must find ways to focus more on the quality of publications and less on the volume of faculty output. Libraries must come together to more intelligently and collaboratively negotiate the purchase of scholarly publications. We face a very dysfunctional market where an expensive good at the institutional level is celebrated as a free good at the user level. We must rethink the matter of intellectual property ownership and the absence of financial interest for universities in the retention of rights for use of the publications produced by their faculties. We must explore the location of quality marking and ways to separate publication from faculty communication and assessment. And we must invest in new electronic scholarly publishing strategies.

The library is central to the academic server model of scholarly publishing. This proposes that universities obtain the newly prepared research papers from their faculties and make them available over the global network, or take responsibility for posting the work of scholars from around the world in selected disciplines. The prestigious publishing model calls upon the scholarly societies and university presses to bring electronic scholarly publishing into the mainstream and to recapture an expanding portion of faculty output. A third model would be the forging of a university publishing cooperative that could compete with the expensive commercial publishers. A prominent example is the newly formed Scholarly Publishing and Academic Resources Coalition or SPARC coming out of the Association of Research Libraries. This initiative seeks to:

- create a more competitive marketplace for research information by providing opportunities for new publishing ventures
- encourage innovative uses of technology to improve scholarly communication
- advance new publishing models as appropriate applications of Internet-2
- promote academic values of access to information for purposes of teaching and research
- advance the continuation of fair use in the electronic environment

The academic library community is advancing a vision of scholarly publishing which aligns with ARL's objectives:

- Foster a competitive market for scholarly publishing by providing realistic alternatives to prevailing commercial publishing options.
- Develop policies for intellectual property management emphasizing broad and easy distribution and reuse of materials.
- Encourage innovative applications of available information technology to enrich and expand available means for distributing research and scholarship.
- Assure that new channels of scholarly communication sustain quality requirements and contribute to promotion and tenure processes.
- Enable the permanent archiving of research publications and scholarly communication in digital formats.

What is truly revolutionary about the explosion in connectivity and digital storage challenging our collection development efforts is the possibility to unbundle information from its physical carrier. In this environment, the most vulnerable organizations are those currently providing information that could be delivered more effectively and inexpensively electronically. We are experiencing a fundamental shift in the economics of information, and it will require changes in the structure of the library industry and in the ways libraries compete for resources and political support. And it will require advancing a new business culture, a new entrepreneurial imperative, where business plans, venture capital, and market competition are blended with academic excellence and research productivity.

In Salmon Rushdie's book, *Haroun and the Sea of Stories*, there is a character named the Water Genie who says the following: "Because the stories were held in fluid form, they retained the ability to change, to become new versions of themselves, to join up with other stories, and so become yet other stories." This is the challenge of the academic library and its collection development program . . . to confront the changing library environment and scholarly landscape with creativity and commitment and to remain focused on our priority goals: to respond to the current and anticipate the future information needs of our community, to collect and organize and service and preserve resources, whether print or electronic, for future generations of students and scholars, and to advance a climate of intellectual freedom.

By the Dawn's Early Light

Milton T. Wolf

Like Francis Scott Key watching the attack on Fort McHenry, I wonder if librarians will ever realize the information power of *"e pluribus unum."* While we ostensibly sing the song and talk the talk of hanging together, we, in fact, more often hang separately when it comes to collection development cooperation. As one wag recently observed, partnership is often another word for seeking funding from some outside agency. And once we get the money, we frequently go our own ways–until the next funding proposal or consortial agreement promises some more of the money pie.

Libraries, in the main, are *not* for-profit institutions! And if you're operating totally like a bottom-line enterprise, you're probably downsizing the intellectual content of your collections not because of a lack of money, or even inefficient use of the little that you have, but because of a lack of vision, because you probably outsourced all those responsibilities which *are* the core of a not-for-profit library.

We are guilty of schooling several generations of librarians in the belief that one collection, if properly developed, could serve all the needs of its clientele locally–with an occasional foray into interlibrary loan. The unfortunate result of this hubris is that library collections are becoming more homogenous as the acquisition dollars buy less and less of the same *"essential"* (read: *TIME, NEWSWEEK, U.S. NEWS AND WORLD REPORT, TV GUIDE, JOURNAL OF* BLAH, BLAH, BLAH) materials.

Milton T. Wolf is Vice President for Collection Development at The Center for Research Libraries.

[Haworth co-indexing entry note]: "By the Dawn's Early Light." Wolf, Milton T. Co-published simultaneously in *Journal of Library Administration* (The Haworth Information Press, an imprint of The Haworth Press, Inc.) Vol. 28, No. 1, 1999, pp. 19-32; and: *Collection Development in a Digital Environment* (ed: Sul H. Lee) The Haworth Information Press, an imprint of The Haworth Press, Inc., 1999, pp. 19-32. Single or multiple copies of this article are available for a fee from The Haworth Document Delivery Service [1-800-342-9678, 9:00 a.m. - 5:00 p.m. (EST). E-mail address: getinfo@haworthpressinc.com].

In short, our clientele have been put on a core starvation diet, deprived of those nutritious sources which distinguish one library from another, those materials which enable thinking outside the box of commercially purveyed pablum that we are all collecting religiously. If we do not understand our need, nay our duty, to build cooperatively complementary collections, we will be guilty of serving up the same old Elsevier mind food for good little boys and girls. This fast-food collecting syndrome, which focuses on the core at the expense of the periphery, is reducing us to the golden arches of the McLibrary, found now at many sites in the US of A!

It's true that we didn't get to this pitiful situation all by ourselves. No, we have been moved briskly and brusquely along the new information corridors by big publishing, big brother, and an antiquated academic system of "publish or perish" which has lost much of its intellectual integrity to the commercial market place. In a recent article entitled "The Politics of Cultural Authority," Wayne A. Wiegand, professor at the University of Wisconsin/Madison School of Library and Information Studies, remarks upon the relationship between knowledge, as it is commercially packaged, and power. He says:

> In the past 20 years or so an army of critical theorists (Michel Foucault, Sandra Harding, Henry Louis Gates Jr., and Pierre Bourdieu, for example) have been questioning the whole concept of "objective" knowledge, and analyzing connections between power and the values assigned to knowledge in its different forms. What they have discovered is that knowledge in any form is never disinterested, never totally objective, and that a discernible link exists between power and the kinds of knowledge people consider most valuable. Because knowledge is never disinterested, powerful people with a vested interest in certain kinds of knowledge work hard to elevate that knowledge to a privileged position. There, they believe, it will have the best chance to influence everyone else.[1]

There are at least two points to glean from this quote: (1) In the present milieu of "cultural authority," librarians are considered merely "handlers of information products" having very little to do with determining the value of those products. (This is why a librarian is seldom appointed the Librarian of Congress, and why the article by Nicholson Baker in the *New Yorker* brought down the wrath of the elite establishment of political correctness upon the keepers of the books.)

The second point about our role in the present cultural and political hierarchy is that librarians are not only considered just handlers of information products but we are also relegated to the fringes, at best, of the academic enterprise which is largely a commercial empire involving publishers, government and scientists (ranked in order of their importance). Jim Davis, formerly the Western Regional Director for Computer Professionals for Social Responsibility, puts it this way:

When profitability becomes the determining factor in the knowledge production (research and development) and information distribution, society loses something. If information can't turn a profit, it won't be developed or stored, regardless of its social value. The president of commercial database vendor Dialog was quoted in 1986 as saying "We can't afford an investment in databases that are not going to earn their keep and pay back their development costs." When asked what areas were not paying their development costs, he answered, "Humanities." And our universe shrinks in the process. Pharmaceuticals (information products) comprise a more dramatic example–for instance, a 1991 World Health Organization report lamented the fact that development of new tuberculosis-fighting drugs all but stopped 25 years ago (even though three million die every year from the disease) because the drugs are "not a big profit maker."[2]

It's not just the Humanities that suffer (although wearing a hair shirt in such disciplines is de rigueur), it's the whole scientific establishment, as well as society in general. The fierce competition engendered in the sciences to get those grants and publish has actually led to secrecy rather than sharing of information. Don't be duped by the fact that the scientists "have to publish," for most of what they publish is old hat to those in the know and is merely done because of the academic reward system and the corporate publishing infrastructure that calls the tune of research.

In truth, there is a well-entrenched, global commercial monopoly on the distribution and approval of ideas. "Content" has become what our commercial enterprises define and distribute. Throughout history, this bottom-line thinking has basically re-enforced status quo intellectuality and knee-jerk responses to social problems. Just as monarchy seldom resulted in philosopher-kings, bottom-line thinking, in which the content is already pre-determined by the distributors, is unlikely to lead to a healthy and diverse society of respectful dissent–not to mention a more democratic forum of critical examination of ideas. The historical parallel of the medieval Church's control of the printed word is obvious and foreboding.

What does all this have to do with the challenges of collection development? Quite a lot, in fact. No less a personage than Ann Okerson in her introductory synopsis to the useful study prepared for the Andrew W. Mellon Foundation entitled *University Libraries and Scholarly Communication* says:

> In scholarly practice today, rights are commonly assigned to publishers, in return for the substantial contribution they make to scholarly communication, while the rewards expected by the scholars themselves are those of prestige, rank, and institutional compensation. . . .[3]

She further states:

> Libraries and publishers already play multiple roles. Libraries and publishers as we now know them are institutions created in and for the technology of the printed, or at least the written, word, depending on information to be produced, distributed, and possessed as a collection of material objects. But it is also critical to realize that both libraries and publishers play other parts as well. Publishers, for example, function as gate-keepers to the world of scholarly communication in managing scholars' and researchers' peer review, which in turn determines what is printed and what is not. Libraries, in turn, have collection development and management functions, but they also serve as indexers and pathfinders for information they do not own. Already such a model departs from the "just-in-case" approach to acquisition and approaches a "just-in-time" model, where material is acquired as it is needed. There may be some blurring in the distinctions among the historical roles of publishers as producers, vendors as intermediaries, and librarians as archivists.[4]

Indeed, there will be some blurring of the roles! There already are and more are in the digital offing; in fact, it is up to us to help determine the new digital dispensation, and we would do well to understand our historical role and how we arrived, without ceremony, where we are now. Librarianship is no longer for the feint of heart, and if we don't learn to work more cooperatively, we will be hung separately by an economic-political juggernaut that is as relentless as it is blind. If we are going to see more clearly, we will have to envision and enact our future roles differently than in the past.

The Mellon Foundation report makes it clear that the "viability of the traditional model of the library" is unlikely to meet the information needs of the emerging global village and its telecommunications technologies. The continued escalation of the prices of library materials, especially those generated by the monopolistic, commercial science publishers, coupled with the expanding number of publications available each year would bankrupt even the biggest budgets from the glory years of the 1960s and early 1970s. Add to this the fact that most libraries in the past two decades have received a smaller share of the overall expenditures budgets of their parent institutions, and it comes as a surprise to no one that libraries are acquiring a declining share of what is being published in the world market. If the traditional concept of creating and maintaining large self-sufficient collections is not yet dead, it is only waiting on the arrival of the taxidermist for the *coup de grace.*

Again, Ann Okerson sums it up and enumerates some possible remedies:

> In the face of this pricing crisis, libraries have responded essentially by redistributing their resources, a mode of response that cannot go on indefinitely. Instead there is a growing realization that no research institution can hope to sustain a self-sufficient collection into the indefinite future. Even before the "crisis," libraries were actively collaborating and sharing resources. Under the circumstances described in the study, and even absent new technologies, libraries would have been led to pursue "without walls" philosophies energetically. With technological hopes rising, possible contributions to mitigation of the "crisis" can come from a combination of:
>
> 1. modification of the academic reward system that drives proliferation of publication.
> 2. possible reduction of first-copy costs by publishers' application of technological advances.

3. savings through use of electronic technologies in distributing and storing information.
4. accelerated resource sharing.
5. perhaps even alterations in the law of intellectual property governing "published" material.[5]

All of these points are well taken and some action is already discernible in each of these areas; however, it seems to me that the one which we should be devoting our utmost attention to is "accelerated resource sharing." In the other arenas of "modifying the academic reward system," the "reduction of publisher costs by technological advances, including savings through our own use of electronic technologies," and "alterations in the intellectual property laws," we are, at best, minor players. And, these arenas are less likely to be susceptible to immediate change as they are part and parcel of an entrenched, profit-motivated cartel that historically has had more success in killing the geese that lay golden eggs rather than husbanding them.

Not to belabor the point, but the Academic Research Factory is so entwined with and beholden to the commercial scientific publishers that we can do little in this arena to effect meaningful change. In a recent article in the professorial magazine *ACADEME* entitled "What Is An Author?" neuropathologist William Rosenblum discussed why scientists publish and the perils and pitfalls of the present system. "Today, at least in the sciences," he begins, "the conduct of scholarly work depends on one's ability to get grant support. Obtaining grants is tied in part to one's productivity. Productivity is judged not only by the quality of one's papers but also by their quantity."[6] He elaborates on this, saying, "Inevitably, pressures to produce more and publish more lead to the formation of larger research teams; so, too, does the legitimate desire to answer scientific questions and the indisputable fact that modern scientific questions are often too complex to be answered by one person's tools. But reliance on larger and larger teams leads to an increasing inability to detect fraud and control sloppy data gathering."[7]

For libraries the outcome of this Publisher-Government-Sciences Complex is an avalanche of costly publications which we are expected to acquire, organize, store, preserve and make available as fast as the whim of desire requires it (but certainly not less than 48 hours and on the requestor's desk, if you don't mind). The worst of all this is that in the sciences, in particular, by the time it is published it is outdated, archival material and displayed in libraries largely for vanity purposes. Real science meanwhile communicates mostly electronically by means of pretexts and posttexts, integrating comments into an evolving document.

And, if the commercial publishers move to more electronic publishing, there is little reason to believe that they will pass on any cost savings; in fact, right now they are charging us for both the electronic and paper versions, which most of the scientists seem to want as well. As Charles W. Bailey, a recognized authority in library systems, remarked in a thought-piece on the probable impact of scholarly electronic publishing on library space needs:

> Academic libraries want their users to have free access to electronic information anywhere, twenty-four hours a day. Publishers want to ensure that libraries provide electronic information to only faculty, students, or staff. They do not want academic libraries to undercut sales by distributing electronic information to other potential customers, such as local businesses. Technological methods for effectively restricting access to electronic information are immature, creating problems for both publishers and libraries. However, in the future, electronic commerce systems may be employed that encrypt information and allow varying fees for different types of access (e.g., view; view and print; or view, print, and store). These systems may give publishers a far higher degree of control over electronic information than they currently exercise over print information.[8]

Bailey goes on to argue that at least in the near term the creation of digital libraries will increase space needs due to the required user work stations, printers, computer and network servers and other expensive technological infrastructure upon which it is based. He then insightfully suggests that "Copyright is the foundation of the existing publishing system. Without difficult-to-reach consensus about how the rights of readers and publishers can be fairly balanced in the electronic environment, scholarly electronic publishing will not be an adequate substitute for print publishing."[9]

And for those pollyanna technonerds who assure you that there will be cost savings because of computerization, the research to date argues against such a sanguine, if not deceitful, view. Much to the chagrin of the computerholics, the overall productivity of U.S. industry during the past twenty years, a period of massive institutionalization of computer systems, has actually decreased slightly. That the computer has changed how we work in libraries cannot be denied, that it has encouraged constant reorganization as we all hurry to fit in with the machines' new bells and whistles (euphemistically called "re-tooling," or staff training), that it now accounts for the most significant outlay of increasing expenditures in most organizations, that a burgeoning group of computer tenders and tweakers (known as Systems Staff) continues to grow, and that, as Emerson maintained, "things are in the saddle and ride mankind" seem all too true.

With all our new technology, the most recent study of interlibrary loan done by the Association of Research Libraries came to the conclusion that even though volume is up over 50%, there has been no significant change during the last decade in the two-week turnaround time for getting books and information between libraries!

So while I agree with Ann Okerson about the nature of the "crisis" facing libraries, I have reservations about how much we can change the academic reward system, the publishers' monopoly, alterations in the law of intellectual property governing "published" material, or how much financial savings (in terms of acquiring more library materials) we will derive from the use of electronic technologies in distributing and storing information.

When looked at closely, all of these problems are a direct result of the Publisher/Government/Sciences Complex, which is already in the initial stages of self-destructing. If anything, we can help it resurrect itself to fulfill its important and vital role of promoting the "Progress of Science and Useful Arts." Competitiveness in science ultimately begets secrecy, secrecy ultimately begets monopoly, and secrecy and monopoly in pursuit of profits and rewards begets laws to ensure its continuance. When copyright law becomes a barrier to the exchange of information and can be used as a monopolistic club to fend off competition, the stagnation that follows inevitably kills the goose that lays the golden eggs. Information does want to be free and like the brain drain prior to World War II where thinkers flocked to the more liberal environment of the United States, ideas will seek new shelter if we do not treat them well.

Do not be surprised if the World Wide Web, that international agora, does not spawn some entrepreneurial types who start selling information that is really useful and relevant to its clients "by the drink," so to speak. With the academy locked into spewing out all this quantity of data, people will willingly pay for just the information that they need. This scenario will also force the Big Publishers actually to compete in the marketplace and to winnow out the present chaff they are guilty of printing. As Charles Bailey indicated, it seems likely that in the near future commerce systems will "allow varying fees for different types of access (e.g., view; view and print; or view, print and store)." As librarians we should encourage a more discriminating use of information, that is our forte and we should do all that we can to promote this aspect of our professional expertise.

The explosion of information works in our favor: almost everyone is now burping up information junk. There is data, data everywhere, but not a lot to think. As Sue Myburgh, a senior lecturer at the University of South Australia, notes in her essay on "information retrieval vs. data retrieval":

> This dichotomy is situated in the encounter that takes place between the information retrievalists, on the one hand, and the data retrievalists, on the other; those who labor with qualitative research methods, as against those to whom quantitative research is all.[10]

Put another way:

> The field of information retrieval can be divided along the lines of its system-based and user-based concerns. While the system-based view is concerned with efficient search techniques to match query and document representation, the user-based view must account for the cognitive state of the searcher and the problem solving context.[11]

Both methods require sophisticated knowledge of the information universe, but the user-based one is a tailored process, as unique as the individual; and it is in this arena that most librarians excel. This is our turf, our metier, our future. Forget the personal trainer, the personal banker, it's the personal bibliographer that everyone will want! It's "content" that people will pay for gladly by the drink, and we are superbly placed to repackage and present information, making it accessible to those who require it.

So let's not get caught up with the behemoth Publisher/Government/Complex. They are already burying their heads in the information morass that they have unwittingly created. By the time they get it straightened out, we can be even further down the information road, doing what we do best: building the world's best library. Notice that I said, the "world's best library" because we are going to learn how to cooperate, collaborate and partner the "best" content ever before put together on this floating ball called Earth.

This is not to say that we should not lobby for modifications to the present political/economic structure, to point out the fallacies of such information legerdemain, to educate our clientele about the intricacies and the vested interests of the "crisis," but we should be spending more time, the majority of our time, doing that which we can do, should do, and, if done well, would ameliorate considerably the "crisis" we face–not to mention the goodwill we would accrue with our users. Collaboration is not just a front for getting grants or making consortial purchases; it is not a buzz word, it's a life style. Collaborators don't care who's on top. Collaboration means "sharing" control–sometimes even not being in control. And what is this craven need we seem to have for autonomy? And where has it actually gotten us? Pretty little research libraries all in a row, looking the same high and low.

While I don't know all the ways we can learn to share, I do know that we could do a lot more than we are doing–and it's less expensive in the long run than the pernicious game we are playing now of one-upmanship. It reminds me of that old parable about the various body parts arguing about which is more important. They all are important and must work in harmony, just like we should be doing. The sum of our parts is greater than any one of us. We are building one grand library, and it's time we became conscious of this and moved with that purpose.

One of the greatest libraries, the Library of Congress, still makes major collecting decisions, like deciding no longer to collect comprehensively in certain areas, without alerting the rest of us in a timely manner. There are innumerable collections scattered across this country and the world, that we have little or no knowledge of. There are magnificent collections rotting in basements, attics and closets that would enrich our national heritage and broaden the content that we could offer our clientele if we would only learn to work more closely together–and select, even locally, less of the detritus belched up by the commercial publishers. With a little more cohesion, we could even influence these bottom-line enterprises to publish what our clients really need, maybe even support some new publishers who were more in tune with content, society, and, heaven knows, civilization.

Cooperative collection development in theory and practice has important ramifications affecting local collection development and management, resource sharing, public services, interlibrary loan, document delivery, and the goal of universal access to information. Its ultimate objective is to maximize the materials to which clientele have access while minimizing local budget expenditures. Surely, this alone can serve as a blueprint for the journey we must embark upon if we are to hang together.

If we truly understand that no one library can satisfy all its users' needs for information, can we overcome our competitive heritage that makes us proud to have more books than someone else even though we are acquiring less and less content? Martin Runkle, Director of the University of Chicago Library, laments our collective inability to cooperate, saying: "The grand schemes don't accomplish as desired for a variety of reasons. Chief among the reasons is that serious and broad-based coordinated collection development that implies some deliberate diminution of local collections clashes with deeply felt needs within academic institutions, particularly the research universities."[12]

Well, we may have finally arrived at that crossroads where not relinquishing some of our local control to pursue the common good means that we are denying our constituents less information than they otherwise would have while, at the same time, supporting a publishing monopoly that gives us more and more useless data. Approximately 2 percent of today's publishers account for 75 percent of U.S. titles produced. (And if you are not sure who they are, look at your approval plans!)

The best summation I can provide you is from a recent article in *Information Technology and Libraries* by Jordan M. Scepanski, Senior Advisor for Library Affairs at the California State University:

> Among the first steps that can be taken in re-thinking how service to the public is rendered is for librarians to assert their professional expertise. The obvious problem with information today is its overabundance. There is more of it than can be handled. Peter Lyman, of the University of California at Berkeley, has pointed out that libraries originally were created to deal

with the problem of information scarcity; that is, to bring together in one place, for the use of the many, items that were few in number so that they could be shared. Now there is too much rather than too little. There also is too much of too little. That is, so much of the information that is overwhelming everyone is of poor quality or of little value. There is a lot that is of little consequence. If the traditional library, then, was the answer to a paucity of information, the new librarian is the solution to its plenitude. There has never been a more critical need for the talents of professionals who not only know how to find information, but how also to evaluate it. The role of the librarian can no longer be one of pointing the way for the user, nor even of just teaching that user how to find what is needed. The librarian must now teach both how to find what is needed and how to assess what is found. Librarians are information experts, and that expertise extends beyond knowing where to look for things. Librarians do know how to differentiate good data from bad, current information from that which is dated, reliable sources from those that are less so. And given the intense subject specializations of content experts–most especially faculty members at universities–and their subsequently narrowly drawn knowledge of their fields, coupled with the extraordinary expansion of scholarship in every field, good librarians frequently know the literature of a given discipline better than many of its practitioners and teaching and research experts. To change public service librarians have to be recognized as information experts and accept that they are so. No longer can they, or society, heed that old admonition, drilled into so many in library schools, that librarians don't make judgments about the information they help people find. If they don't make such judgments no one will, and clients will be the worse for librarian timidity. The profession should return to the public librarian's approach of an earlier era, that of the "reader's advisor," the librarian whose knowledge of the disciplines and of their literature and of the reader's interest and needs allowed functioning as a guide and a counselor. Librarians once again need to guide and counsel. They need to advise and to teach.[13]

It is time for us to re-dedicate ourselves to the value-added things we bring to the information arena, to re-engineer our Farmington plans, to develop a national/international conspectus for our global library, to preserve the recorded knowledge of civilization, to put our always limited funds toward our overarching visions: to ensure that we have cooperative just-in-case repositories to serve the just-in-time needs of our clientele.

Over the years it has become almost a cliche to urge people to "think globally, act locally." Could we possibly add a parenthetical addendum to "act locally (with global intent)"? After all, whether you realize it or not, we are building a global collection. And you are one of its personal bibliographers!

NOTES

1. Wayne A. Wiegand. "The Politics of Cultural Authority," *American Libraries* 29 (January 1998): 81.
2. Jim Davis. "The Incompatibility of Capitalism and Information," *Intertek* 3.4 (1993): 19.
3. Ann Okerson, Synopsis to University Libraries and Scholarly Communication by Anthony M. Cummings et al. (The Association of Research Libraries for the Andrew W. Mellon Foundation, November 1992), p. xxvii.
4. Ibid.
5. Ibid., p. xxii.
6. William I. Rosenblum. "What Is an Author? The Responsibilities of Authorship," *Academe* 83 (November-December 1997): 34.
7. Ibid., p. 37.
8. Charles W. Bailey, "Bricks, Bytes or Both?" in *Information Imagineering: Meeting at the Interface*, eds. Milton T. Wolf, Pat Ensor, and Mary Augusta Thomas Chicago: American Library Association, 1998), pp. 90–91.
9. Ibid., p. 94.
10. Sue Myburgh. "The Clash of the Titans: Information Retrieval vs. Data Retrieval," in *Information Imagineering: Meeting at the Interface*, eds. Milton T. Wolf, Pat Ensor, and Mary Augusta Thomas (Chicago: American Library Association, 1998), pp. 53-54.
11. Ibid., p. 54.
12. Martin Runkle. "What Was the Original Mission of The Center for Research Libraries and How Has It Changed?" (Chicago: CRL Symposium, April 25, 1997), p. 2.
13. Jordan M. Scepanski. "Public Services in a Telecommuting World," *Information Technology and Libraries* 15 (March 1966): 44.

WORKS CITED

Bailey, Charles W. "Bricks, Bytes or Both?" in *Information Imagineering: Meeting at the Interface*, pp. 89-99. Edited by Milton T. Wolf, Pat Ensor, and Mary Augusta Thomas. Chicago: American Library Association, 1998.
Cummings, Anthony M.; Witte, Marcia L.; Bowen, William G.; Lazarus, Laura O.;

and Ekman, Richard H. *University Libraries and Scholarly Communication.* Synopsis by Ann Okerson. The Association of Research Libraries for the Andrew W. Mellon Foundation, November 1992.

Davis, Jim. "The Incompatibility of Capitalism and Information," *Intertek* 3.4 (1993): 18-21.

Myburgh, Sue. "The Clash of the Titans: Information Retrieval vs. Data Retrieval," in *Information Imagineering: Meeting at the Interface,* pp. 50-61. Edited by Milton T. Wolf, Pat Ensor, and Mary Augusta Thomas. Chicago: American Library Association, 1998.

Rosenblum, William I. "What Is an Author? The Responsibilities of Authorship," *Academe* 83 (November-December 1997): 34-37.

Runkle, Martin. "What Was the Original Mission of The Center for Research Libraries and How Has It Changed?" pp. 2-5. Symposium on "CRL's Role in the Emerging Global Resource Program," Hotel Sofitel, Chicago, April 25, 1997.

Scepanski, Jordan M. "Public Services in a Telecommuting World," *Information Technology and Libraries* 15 (March 1966): 41-44.

Wiegand, Wayne A. "The Politics of Cultural Authority," *American Libraries* 29 (January 1998): 80-82.

Collection Development
and Professional Ethics

Kenneth Frazier

It's easy to understand why we cringe at the introduction of ethical considerations into professional problem-solving. The great lexicographer Samuel Johnson, Tory Christian and defender of the Anglican faith though he was, included in his prayers that God might spare him from his *"scruples"* and grant him a *"willingness to be pleased."*[1]

Johnson's remark is grounded in the reality of everyday experience. Life presents us with enough difficulties without the added burden of being ethically fastidious in our work. Focusing on the moral considerations of any job violates the generally advisable strategy of not taking work too personally.

After all, ethical discourse introduces the great likelihood of moral disapproval of some, attribution of base motives to others, and sanctimonious claims of moral superiority, usually for ourselves. With good reason, we worry that talking about such things will cause resentment, impede constructive communication, and create barriers between people who must do business with each other over the long haul.

However, for librarianship in a time of transformative change in scholarly communication the ethical dilemmas of collection development are inescapable. When librarians make forced choices with limited resources or sign institutional licenses for access to electronic infor-

---

Kenneth Frazier is Director of the General Library System at the University of Wisconsin in Madison, WI.

[Haworth co-indexing entry note]: "Collection Development and Professional Ethics." Frazier, Kenneth. Co-published simultaneously in *Journal of Library Administration* (The Haworth Information Press, an imprint of The Haworth Press, Inc.) Vol. 28, No. 1, 1999, pp. 33-46; and: *Collection Development in a Digital Environment* (ed: Sul H. Lee) The Haworth Information Press, an imprint of The Haworth Press, Inc., 1999, pp. 33-46. Single or multiple copies of this article are available for a fee from The Haworth Document Delivery Service [1-800-342-9678, 9:00 a.m. - 5:00 p.m. (EST). E-mail address: getinfo@haworthpressinc.com].

33

mation, we make decisions with serious ethical implications for library users as well as for our institutions. We may choose to ignore the ethical aspects of these decisions, but the ethical consequences are there in any case.

In this paper I will illustrate the ethical dilemmas of library collection development as they are playing out in three contemporary examples:

- Litigation by the publisher Gordon & Breach against Professor Henry H. Barschall, the American Institute of Physics, and the American Physical Society.
- The unsuccessful attempt by the editors of *The History of European Ideas* to move their journal from Elsevier publishers to MIT Press.
- The ongoing effort by publishers to use licensing contracts to abolish interlibrary loan services for information in electronic formats.

All three of these examples have emerged from the turbulent environment of technological, economic, and legal developments that has come to be called the scholarly communication crisis. At the risk of oversimplifying a complex set of issues, the dynamics of the crisis are driven by the following forces:

- Continued growth in scholarly publication in all formats
- Extraordinary inflation in the cost of published materials
- Static, and in some cases declining, funding for library resources
- Consolidation of the information industries
- Continued reliance on slow, expensive publishing methods
- Emerging models of electronic scholarly communication
- Surrender of copyright ownership by scholars and researchers
- Efforts by publishers to change international copyright laws

These developments are interrelated and, when taken together, amount to a trend toward an increasingly expensive scholarly communication system which is governed by a more restrictive copyright law and largely under the control of multinational information conglomerates. This is not an inevitable outcome but one which depends on the continuing passivity of university and research institutions with respect to the management and ownership of information that they produce. A much different range of possible futures for scholarly communication is possible if researchers, librarians and academic administrators give due consideration to the ethical significance of institutional decisions that affect public access to information. No matter what their wealth or size, publishers do not create nor sponsor the creation of the intellectual property that they distribute. Consequently, scholars and research institutions are free to create new modes of scholarly communication. Given that authors working in an electronic environment can communicate directly with their audiences, electronic publishing introduces the real possibility of *disintermediation*, that is, the elimination of intermediaries in the process of editing, certifying, organizing, distributing, and archiving published materials. It is difficult to envision any future model of digital scholarly communication in which some amount of disintermediation will not occur–the only real question is how, and in whose interests, these new distribution systems will be organized.

THE RELEVANCE OF PROFESSIONAL ETHICS

The Statement on Professional Ethics (adopted by ALA Council, June 1981, revised 1995) concludes with the following words:

> We [librarians] significantly influence or control the selection, organization, preservation, and dissemination of information. In a political system grounded in an informed citizenry, librarians are members of a profession explicitly committed to intellectual freedom and the freedom of access to information. We have a special obligation to ensure the free flow of information and ideas to present and future generations.[2]

What are we to make of this ethical declaration? Paul R. Camenisch, the author of a remarkable essay entitled "On being a professional, morally speaking," rightly points out that no matter what professional societies really intend in creating codes of ethics, professionals should not be surprised that the public takes the core ethical commitment seriously and expects some degree of accountability.

Even if we were to agree that these pronouncements are utterly insincere, the ethical obligation of the professions to the public would not disappear if professional codes of ethics were abolished. Professional education and many of the institutions in which professionals work are supported with public resources. Consequently, the moral obligation of professionals is not strictly a personal one to provide competent service, protect privacy, and not exploit clients. It is also the responsibility of the profession to society generally, recognizing that the wider community sustains the professions and depends on them for the ethical performance of essential services.

For librarians, this concept is explicitly stated in the ethical code. Librarians not only have the responsibility to provide users with the best possible library services, but they also have a responsibility to society to maintain a knowledge management system that maximizes the public interest in the "free flow of information" and distributes the benefits of information access as democratically as possible.

For all practicing professionals this ethical responsibility to society introduces the potential ethical dilemma of situations in which the wishes of clients may be at variance, or even in conflict, with the public good. Admittedly, it is an exceedingly rare event when professionals allow public interests to compete with the bread-and-butter imperative to serve their primary clientele. However, it is also a legitimate measure of professional authority when a client accepts a professional's judgment that the public will benefit by some adjustment in the client's expectations.

In a wonderful book by William M. Sullivan entitled *Work and Integrity*, this central ethical dilemma of professionalism is summarized as follows: "The client often depends on the wisdom and integrity of the professional's judgement. The professional, on the other hand, cannot be simply the client's tool or instrument. The professional is accountable *to* the client as to whether the professional is serving the client's best interests, but the professional is also accountable *for* the public purpose for which the profession exists."[3]

It is this fundamental insight that provides the context for the discussion of the ethical cases that follow.

DEALING WITH GORDON & BREACH: A PROBLEM OF "CLEAN HANDS"

The so-called "clean hands" dilemma typically arises when a professional is asked to provide services for a client whose conduct, while legal, is so ethically reprehensible that the professional would prefer to have no dealings with this person. The problem for librarians in dealing with the publisher Gordon & Breach is significantly different in that it is library users who want and need access to the journals produced by a publisher that has engaged in a systematic effort to suppress free expression and legitimate academic inquiry.

A more complete account of the litigation by Gordon & Breach (G&B) against Professor Henry Barschall and the American Institute of Physics/American Physical Society is available at http://barschall. stanford.edu. For purposes of this discussion, the essential facts can be quickly sketched as follows.

In December 1986, Professor Henry Barschall, an *emeritus* physics professor at the University of Wisconsin-Madison, compared the cost of physics journals by calculating the cost-per-thousand-characters of content and published his findings in tabular form with an accompanying article in *Physics Today*. After the article came out Gordon & Breach wrote to Barschall and APS complaining that there were errors in the survey and requested that G&B be eliminated from any future surveys.

In 1988, Barschall published a more comprehensive version of the study, this time covering over 200 physics journals which also combined his cost per kilocharacter methodology with the so-called "impact factor" which was published by *Science Citation Index*.[4] By combining these two measures, Barschall created a cost/impact ratio which he described as "perhaps the most significant measure of the cost effectiveness of the journal."

In Barschall's studies the physics journals published by Gordon & Breach were shown to be substantially more expensive than many other physics journals, including those published by APS/AIP. After the publication of the 1988 study, Gordon & Breach wrote again, this time to AIP, demanding a retraction.

When AIP and APS refused to retract or otherwise repudiate the Barschall studies, G&B filed suit in Swiss, French, and West German courts in July 1989 on the grounds that the articles were not really studies of the cost of physics journals but, rather, advertisements for AIP and APS journals which unfairly denigrated the competition, specifically the journals published by Gordon & Breach. A similar lawsuit was filed in the U.S. courts in September 1993 alleging that the Barschall studies were a "literally false advertisement."

The Swiss and German courts decisively rejected G&B's case as well as their subsequent appeals. The French court ruled in G&B's favor. The fact that Barschall's article was obviously not an advertisement, that his findings were correct, and that, in any case, he was entitled to freedom of expression apparently did not hold sway in France. The case is still being appealed.

The ruling of the U.S. Southern District Court of New York gave Barschall and AIP/APS a nearly total victory, lacking significantly the recovery of the immense legal expense of defending fundamental academic freedoms. Judge Leonard Sand's opinion is lively, logical, and concludes with the following strong endorsement of academic freedom: "If G&B believes that librarians will make more optimal decisions if they consider information other than that provided by defendants, its solution is to augment rather than censor the available truthful information."

The Court found that Barschall's methodology was valid and his conclusions true. The journals published by professional societies are, in fact, a relative bargain compared to many commercial publications. The Court also observed that the evidence presented in the trial demonstrated that "regardless of the measure used, G&B's consistently scored at the bottom."

Henry Barschall emerged as a hero of the academic community by maintaining his dignity and integrity throughout years of legal harassment by G&B. He refused to be intimidated by the personal attack on his character and motives.

However, Gordon & Breach succeeded in accomplishing some of their purposes. The volley of lawsuits in four different countries scared the wits out of the scholarly community. The cost of defending this many legal cases was so ruinously expensive that few non-profit organizations could begin to imagine carrying the kind of financial burden that was inflicted on AIP/APS. It was impossible even to contemplate a journal cost study of scientific journals without feeling the pressure of the G&B litigation. Authors and publishers were cowed into excluding G&B journals from their research. The chill on free academic inquiry into the cost of scientific journals continues to this day. At the time of this writing G&B is still appealing the case.

The evidence presented during the District Court case also substantiated serious ethical concerns about G&B's conduct:

- G&B refused to play by the accepted rules of academic discourse by rejecting reasonable opportunities to offer their own evidence on the issue of journal costs in the same journals that had originally published Barschall's studies and, instead, sought to suppress the academic freedom of others.

- G&B conducted a sustained, global campaign to silence any adverse comment on the cost and value of their journals in a blatant assault on freedom of expression.
- G&B and its allies engaged in unwarranted personal attacks on the integrity and motives of a respected researcher.

Henry Barschall did not live to see the vindication of his work by the U.S. District Court. He died of cancer in February 1997. The personal attacks on him continued after the court ruling. As recently as January 1998, Albert Henderson, the ubiquitous apologist for and sometime employee of Gordon & Breach, in an opinion piece entitled "Lawful Misconduct" (*The Scientist*, January 19, 1998) described Barschall's studies as "containing errors, perhaps intentional errors."

Months after Barschall's death, Henderson contacted Provost John Wiley of the University of Wisconsin-Madison and, in a telephone conversation with Wiley, inquired why disciplinary action had not been taken against Professor Barschall for his alleged conflict of interest and the errors of his research on the cost of physics journals.

In a news release following the District Court ruling, Gordon & Breach defended its legal action on the grounds that " . . . G&B faced threats and aggressive action in the form of circulated and published articles that used erroneous information to foster boycotts and cancellations of its journals."[5]

In fact, Barschall's studies did not even mention Gordon & Breach by name in the text of the articles, much less recommend cancellation of G&B journals. There is no evidence of any librarian calling for a mass boycott of G&B journals. Regrettably, most research libraries, including the physics library at the University of Wisconsin-Madison, continue to subscribe to G&B journals.

The standard answer to the clean hands dilemma found in law and medicine is that professionals may avoid dealing with a disreputable client by providing an appropriate referral. In similar fashion, librarians can approach the ethical quandary of dealing with Gordon & Breach by proposing alternative methods for library users to gain access to the content of G&B journals. Specifically, librarians should consider the following options:

- Buying G&B journals on the used market,
- Suggesting that researchers subscribe themselves using grant funding,
- Providing document delivery access for library users, paying royalties when necessary, as an alternative to library subscription.

Even if all of these alternatives are unacceptable to library users, librarians would be fulfilling a fundamental obligation to carry out their responsibilities with professional integrity by raising the ethical question with faculty of whether or not it is necessary to continue doing business with Gordon & Breach.

THE CASE OF THE CAPTIVE JOURNAL:
HISTORY OF EUROPEAN IDEAS
BECOMES EUROPEAN LEGACY

In December 1994, the editors of the journal entitled *History of European Ideas* notified their publisher, Elsevier Pergamon, that they were going to seek a new publisher for the journal. The editors board had grown dissatisfied with Elsevier's pricing policies and their overall business relationship with the publisher. After some negotiation, the editors selected MIT Press as the new publisher for *History of European Ideas*, an option that seemed open to them since there was no signed agreement giving Elsevier ownership of the title.

MIT Press soon learned that the absence of a contract would not prevent Elsevier from claiming complete legal ownership of *History of European Ideas*. Not only did Elsevier insist that they owned the title, trademark, and volume numbering of the journal, their legal representatives threatened litigation to prevent MIT Press from describing the new, renamed (now known as *European Legacy*) journal as a "successor journal" to *History of European Ideas*.

MIT Press was stunned by Elsevier's aggressive response. They had assumed, naively perhaps, that an amicable separation was possible given that humanities publishing of this type was not Elsevier's core business, that the journal was a tiny piece of Elsevier's vast empire, and that Elsevier, usually so meticulous with legal details, did not have a contract. However, what had started out as a handshake agreement between people who thought they were colleagues in the shared enterprise of scholarly communication ended with a very ungenteel display of muscle by one of the richest and most powerful publishers in the world. Needless to say, MIT Press was in no position to take on Elsevier in court.

MIT Press faced a daunting task. First of all, they had already made a commitment to publish a great deal of new material, including the proceedings from a major conference. They had no subscriber base. They were forced to market *European Legacy* as an entirely new journal. And, for several years, there would be no significant indexing of the new publication to guide potential users to the contents.

It proved to be an uphill struggle for the new journal. The economic consequence of publishing a fat paper journal for a very thin subscriber list was entirely predictable. *European Legacy* hemorrhaged money. The red ink was such that it undermined the ability of MIT Press to take on other worthy projects.

Given the obstacles, *European Legacy* has made remarkable progress. To their credit, MIT Press did succeed in producing a high quality journal at a reasonable price. The journal now has over 300 subscribers, including 140 institutional subscriptions. It is headed toward the black, but not fast enough. The journal is still losing money and MIT Press cannot afford to carry it for much longer.

Unlike the previous example involving Gordon & Breach, in this case it would be difficult to argue that Elsevier behaved unethically. Even in the absence of a contract, Elsevier was entitled to claim an ownership interest in the journal since Pergamon (which Elsevier later acquired) had undertaken the financial risk of publishing *History of European Ideas* when it was a start-up journal. Having supported the journal until it became profit-making, the publisher could argue, with some justice, that it should not be deprived of a paying property without compensation.

On the other hand, the editors had good reason to be concerned about Elsevier's pricing policies which result in charging more and more to fewer and fewer subscribers. This can, and usually does, ensure that Elsevier journals continue to make money for the publisher, but it virtually guarantees that there will be a continually shrinking readership for the journal. That is, Elsevier's aggressive pricing strategy often defeats the scholarly communication purpose for which a journal exists.

The ethical issue for librarians is whether the scholars who create the intellectual content of journals should be held captive by the practical difficulties of moving a journal, if not its name, to a new publisher. The interests of scholarly communication will be best served if libraries and universities create the conditions to make sure that such a change-of-venue for journals is possible. Although publishers have every right to protect their financial interests with contracts, they are not entitled to the perpetual ownership of the future output of a group of editors and authors.

Therefore, the academic community needs to develop safe havens for journals that offer editors and editorial boards a reasonable opportunity to re-start an existing journal, if necessary, under a new name. The creation of new publishing venues will cost money and it will not be risk free for the sponsoring institutions, but it will improve the climate for scholarly publishing by encouraging commercial publishers to moderate prices and negotiate in good faith with editors–or face the prospect of losing the journal.

LICENSE TO KILL:
CONTRACTING FOR THE DEMISE
OF INTERLIBRARY LOAN

Publishers and database vendors want to do away with interlibrary loan services (ILL) for information in digital format. They believe that, in the future, interlibrary loan services will provide current and potential subscribers to their products with a convenient alternative for gaining free access to the content of electronic journals and databases. As they envision it, the library interloan departments will soon be capable of sending digital copies of an article to any information user, anywhere, who has a properly equipped computer or fax machine.

However, the publishers are not just worried about the potential of interlibrary loan to undermine the primary market for information products. They also want control of all secondary markets for the content of their databases, including the occasional and rare uses of information typically served by interlibrary loan in education and research. Once ILL is dead, publishers will have what they always wanted, i.e., an information system that requires that they are compensated for every single use of copyright-protected information under their control.

Consequently, they have drafted licensing terms for electronic information products which flatly prohibit all interlibrary loan service using the content of electronic databases. In fact, some licenses go so far as to prohibit any distribution of database content to anyone who is not a member of the licensed user community. This contractual language would also outlaw the use of database content in colleague communication outside the institution, all university reference, consulting and outreach services, as well as all interlibrary loan.

It is not just the commercial publishers that have taken this position on interlibrary loan access to electronic library resources. University presses, professional societies, and the Association of American Publishers have gone on record saying that there should be no such thing as interlibrary loan for information in electronic formats.

The effect of these licenses is to replace the plain language of the United States Copyright Law which expressly permits interlibrary loan for library materials in all formats. If librarians are ready to sign licenses that prohibit interlibrary loan, then there is very little purpose in professional library associations devoting so much energy to defending the rights of information users found in Federal copyright law.

The drive to kill off interlibrary loan is all the more remarkable given that there is no evidence that ILL has undermined the market for digital information products. Libraries do not allow direct access to licensed databases for unauthorized users. More importantly, the systematic copying of journal articles for interlibrary loan services, i.e., regular copying that serves as a replacement for subscription-based access to journals, is both illegal under the current copyright law and a violation of professional ethics.

Ironically, the death of ILL will mean less access to information for people of limited means rather than more money for publishers. If librarians agree to these terms, many people (including farmers, high school students, grade school teachers, and small business owners) will be cut off from access to information because they simply can't afford the prices charged by commercial information vendors. Commercial article access is anything but cheap; per article fees of $10.00 to $25.00 per article are already commonplace. Once publishers succeed in choking off all public interlibrary loan, information consumers will have to pay whatever the publisher demands or get along without it.

Many land-grant and public universities have an explicit mandate to serve as resource libraries for the state or region. This responsibility includes providing access to information for people who have very little money and no access to technology. It will be impossible to fulfill that mission if libraries cannot lend materials from their collections. Universities will no longer be able to represent themselves as the knowledge repositories of the state when all current research is available only to paying customers.

A more likely future scenario if ILL for digital resources is prohibited is that a great deal of information will cease to be available at all after a few years. It is libraries, not publishers, that have always assumed responsibility for preserving knowledge over time. History has shown that publishers can be expected to maintain access to their publications only so long as it is profitable.

More than half of all interlibrary loans from research libraries are for materials that are more than ten years old. Many interlibrary loan requests are for uncommon materials that are difficult to obtain. When publications cease or publishers go out of business, very often the only remaining source of access to the information is interlibrary loan.

The ethical dilemma for librarians is that database licenses that prohibit interlibrary loan will have little or no immediate affect on our primary clientele. Our own students and faculty will probably not care if the university library is prohibited from lending an article to the local high school library. As a growing number of libraries agree to licensing that prohibits interlibrary loan, the pressure on other libraries to accept these terms may become unbearable. To resist will only deny one's own primary clientele access to information.

CONCLUSION

All three of the examples presented here feature the potential of an ethical dilemma of choosing between the immediate needs and preferences of our primary clients and our professional responsibility to optimize public access to knowledge. None of them require unusual or heroic measures in order for librarians to maintain their professional integrity.

In a perfect world, the entire academic community would shun Gordon & Breach, but most research libraries have continued G&B journals because faculty and students need the information they contain. In the case of *European Legacy*, librarians may save this one journal from extinction, but we are unlikely to adopt a general policy of buying only those journals that are produced by publishers who measure up to our ethical ideals. And, as difficult as it is to imagine librarians abandoning their obligation to provide public access to information via interlibrary loan, the library's mandate to supply vital information for faculty and students may overwhelm the secondary mission of libraries to serve the wider public interest.

However, the purpose of professional ethics is not to require people to act as moral exemplars in their work. The professions, perhaps all professions including law, are better at serving as intermediaries in negotiating ethical issues than as advocates representing both clients and the welfare of the public. The truth is, of course, that librarians are not *disinterested* parties in the public policy questions involving access to information. The stakes for everyone are high. What we can do is make the ethical dimension of library decision-making as public and explicit as our circumstances allow.

We librarians can fulfill our professional responsibilities with integrity without entering into an adversarial relationship with library users or with litigious publishers.

First, the central ethical responsibility for librarians is to be honest in describing the alternatives available to our institutions in gaining access to information. For example, it isn't necessary to buy outrageously overpriced journals in order to have access to their contents. Commercial document delivery access is often much less costly than an institutional subscription. At the very least, librarians can stop acting as the on-campus sales force for commercial publishers by insisting that our institutions have "no choice" but to pay whatever the publishers demand.

Secondly, nearly all librarians have some margin of opportunity to use a portion of the library collection budget to support technical innovations in publishing and to encourage new models of scholarly communication. To claim otherwise is simply not credible. The redirection of a small percentage of an acquisitions budget will make an enormous difference in establishing alternative communication products in the marketplace.

And finally, we all have within our power the ability to promote much greater *awareness* of the importance of reasonable access to information in a free society. One of the most valuable insights that has emerged from the environmental movement is that *awareness matters* a very great deal.[6] The real danger is not so much that we will fail to make the correct ethical decision in a particular situation, but that we will disconnect from the reality that we *are* making important ethical decisions about the future availability of knowledge.

The time is ripe to change scholarly communication for the better. If librarians act as wise consumers of information products, encourage technical innovation that benefits information users, and promote public awareness of the importance of open access to information, librarians–like other highly respected professionals–will be recognized and rewarded by society.

NOTES

1. Bate, W. Jackson. *Samuel Johnson*. New York: Harcourt Brace Jovanovich, 1977, p. 381.

2. "ALA Code of Ethics," *American Libraries* 26(7), July/August 1995, p. 673.

3. Sullivan, William M. *Work and Integrity: the Crisis and Promise of Professionalism in America*. New York: HarperBusiness, 1995, p. 43.

4. Barschall, Henry H. and J. R. Arrington. "Cost of Physics Journals: A survey," *Bulletin of the American Physical Society* 33 (1988):1437-47.

5. Gordon & Breach News Release, August 28, 1997 in "Gordon and Breach v. American Institute of Physics and American Physical Society: A briefing packet for ARL directors." Washington, D.C.: Association of Research Libraries, October 1997.

6. Hiss, Tony. *The Experience of Place*. New York: Knopf, 1990, p. xii.

Making the Wild Wind Visible: Information Technology in a Brave New World

Dennis Dillon

Making the wild wind visible is a phrase from the poet Robinson Jeffers. He lived in a stone house on a high bluff overlooking the Pacific in California's Big Sur country. When the ocean winds made contact with the land, they carved the local rock into new and unusual shapes, they drove salt spray up into the hills where it could be smelled miles away, and they created a variety of ever shifting currents in the air below the poet's perch. But none of this was apparent to the casual observer. The winds were invisible and the only way the poet could see them was to watch the hawks as they glided on the currents below. It was the hawks that made the wild wind visible. In a similar vein it is words that make the wild winds of human thought visible. Words that appear in books and journals and nowadays on the World Wide Web.

But what does this new World Wide Web mean for libraries? We know that the Web is vastly different from print. But in what ways? What will it spawn? We can discern a few clues if we examine both the present trends and the past history of information technology. We can expect that the Web, like all new communication technologies, will create and require new roles for the players in the current communications, publishing, and information technology mix. We can expect that

Dennis Dillon is Head of the Collections and Information Resources Division at The University of Texas at Austin in Austin, TX.

[Haworth co-indexing entry note]: "Making the Wild Wind Visible: Information Technology in a Brave New World." Dillon, Dennis. Co-published simultaneously in *Journal of Library Administration* (The Haworth Information Press, an imprint of The Haworth Press, Inc.) Vol. 28, No. 1, 1999, pp. 47-61; and: *Collection Development in a Digital Environment* (ed: Sul H. Lee) The Haworth Information Press, an imprint of The Haworth Press, Inc., 1999, pp. 47-61. Single or multiple copies of this article are available for a fee from The Haworth Document Delivery Service [1-800-342-9678, 9:00 a.m. - 5:00 p.m. (EST). E-mail address: getinfo@haworthpressinc.com].

47

there will be a proliferation of new information products, that the consumer will have a wealth of free information from which to choose, and that the amount of trivia, noise, and de-contextualized information fragments will increase. These are all a continuation of the general effects electronic information technology has had upon society since the first appearance of the telegraph. But none of the implications of current information technology seriously affects the underlying rationale, purpose, or function of the book. As Louis Rossetto, the co-founder of *Wired,* says about the current state of affairs, "The Web is not about reading. It's not about developing long ideas. It's about getting to mission-critical information."[1] For the foreseeable future, the information technology and intellectual construct that is the book, is in no danger from the changes in electronic information technology.

But the information environment is clearly changing and librarians have to settle a few questions if they are to remain viable and play an important role during and after this transition. Among these questions are:

1. What is our vision of the library? What will be the library's focus?
2. What are the library's expectations of its vendors?
3. And as Clifford Lynch, the Executive Director of the Coalition for Networked Information, recently noted, "Digital libraries are dangerous in the sense that in a time when libraries are starved for funding for collections you are diverting a lot of resources away from building collections." The questions he says we must ask ourselves are, "Do digital libraries make a difference, does electronic information make a difference, is it worth the investment?"[2]

These are some of our issues. But does knowing the issues provide any help? As Seneca observed two thousand years ago, "If a man does not know what harbor he is making for, no wind is the right wind."[3] Among the librarians I know, the wind is blowing every which way. They don't know whether to become publishers, distance educators, Webmasters, rare book librarians, trainers, multi-media specialists, contract law lawyers, or whether to just quit and go work for Dutch publishing conglomerates. The winds of change are blowing, but they are not blowing strong enough to push us into a safe harbor. It is not clear in which direction we should be sailing. Perhaps by looking backwards, we can gain a better perspective on our current situation.

In the beginning was the word. As countless cultures have noted, words are nothing but wind, human breaths formed and spoken. Five-thousand years ago we discovered a way to make this wind visible by making cuneiform marks on wet clay. With this simple act human words were no longer writ on the wind, but were preserved through the millennium. We were now able to capture our thoughts and make them visible. Visible not only to ourselves, but also to others across great distances and time. From this combination of wind and earth grew books, and from collections of books grew libraries.

But this new technology of books was not welcomed by everyone. Socrates believed that books would destroy thought, that they would lead to a dumbing down of mankind because they did not allow for the questioning, examining, and probing of the author that were part of the oral tradition. Socrates thought of books much as we think of television, as a new-fangled one-way means of communication in which the reader/viewer was nothing more than a passive recipient of the message. He much preferred the give and take of the Socratic method, which he believed contributed to the rigorous development of the mind in ways that books could not.[4]

In Plato's *Phaedrus* there is a discussion of books in which a god explains his invention of writing to an Egyptian king. The god claims that writing will improve both the wisdom and memory of the Egyptians. The king replies that inventors are not the best judges of the benefits and harm caused by inventions, and that writing will cause those who learn it to cease to exercise their memory and become forgetful.

> They will rely on writing to bring things to their remembrance by external signs instead of their internal resources. What you have discovered is a receipt for recollection, not for memory. And as for wisdom, your pupils will have the reputation for it without the reality: They will receive a quantity of information without proper instruction, and in consequence be thought very knowledgeable when they are for the most part quite ignorant. And because they are filled with the conceit of wisdom instead of real wisdom they will be a burden to society.[5]

From this beginning as a burdensome frivolous tool of the ignorant, we now jump ahead 3,000 years in the history of the book to the fears of George Orwell in *1984* and Aldous Huxley in *Brave New World*. They believed that the book would soon become a forgotten relic of the past. Orwell feared a future in which the book would be banned, information would be scarce, and the truth would be concealed from us. Huxley feared a future in which there would be so much information and entertainment that no one would have any interest in reading a book. He feared that the truth would be drowned in a sea of irrelevance and that people would become addicted to egoism. Of these two visions, Huxley's is the one which most resonates with us today.[6]

Today we might be said to live in an information swamp. A swamp humid with bits and bytes. A swamp slimy with information that plops and slithers; information that swims past your ankles, and drips from the trees above. A swamp so rich with information that it clings to your skin like a wet shirt, buzzes past your ears, gets tangled in your hair, and seeps into your eyes until you find yourself thinking, "Is there no escape?" There is little doubt that a combination of advancing technology and a dramatic increase in the numbers of educated human beings have led to increased communication and an explosion of information of all kinds. Both the process of human discovery and the impulse to communicate are spiraling well beyond the limits of previous human experience. But neither process is new. They existed before universities, before publishers, before the printing press, and before the alphabet. As the Old Testament put it, "Many shall run to and fro, and knowledge shall be increased."[7]

What is new, as one contemporary critic has noted, is that "the capacity to convey and to accumulate knowledge, to record and share experience would seem to have approached a consummation in which every event in the surrounding reality can be captured."[8] As librarians we know that when we wake tomorrow, human beings will have discovered even more information that should be in our libraries, and that by next week libraries will be even further behind in their collecting responsibilities than they are now. Libraries were not designed to handle this situation. Most current libraries are based on a working model conceptualized in the 19th century and are simply not structured to handle the current volume of books, journals, multimedia, and electronic resources. Librarians find themselves constructing parallel but disconnected virtual and physical libraries. Constructing two libraries instead of one, both largely invisible to one another, and both inadequately funded.

Books have done much to create the culture we currently live in. We are not always conscious of the effects books have had on us just as we are not always aware of the air we breathe or the houses we live in. But no information technology is neutral in its affects. Whereas some of our ancestors feared that books would result in the loss of important human traits, Orwell and Huxley lamented the potential loss of reflective thinking, reasoned argument, and analytical power that the linear arrangement of the book imposed. For western man, the written word promoted the comforting notion that the universe was as fixed and unchanging as the words he used to describe it on paper. The notion of an orderly universe that was capable of being analyzed and known helped to promote the manner of thought that led to western science. The printed word with its emphasis on logic, sequence, objectivity, detachment, and discipline, and with the freedom it provides readers to explore written arguments and implications at their own pace is in direct contrast, for example, to television, which emphasizes imagery, narrative, intimacy, immediate gratification, and quick emotional response. A civilization that developed around television as its principle information technology would be far different from a civilization that developed around the written word.

With writing, even the medium on which the words are written can make a difference. The Egyptians found that writing on papyrus was faster than chiseling thoughts onto stone and as a result of this change in medium, written thoughts were composed more quickly; "by escaping the heavy medium of stone thought gained lightness."[9] This in turn resulted in prose of increased interest, observation, and reflection. Writing and books also affected society in deeper ways, creating aristocracies out of those who knew how to write and read, and who therefore had a monopoly on knowledge. It made administration more efficient, led to increased centralization, and became a stepping stone to personal prosperity and career advancement. It also helped to create a library of philosophical options, including belief and support systems that are not available in oral cultures, and eventually leading, some maintain, to the nihilism and egoism observable in western culture.

The information technology of the book has deeply colored the way we think about information and the intellectual constructs we use to model the world. When comparing the book to the World Wide Web, it is easy to note deficiencies in the new technology, but it is not safe to draw too many obvious conclusions about the weaknesses we see with today's networked information. Many of the current structural problems with the World Wide Web are likely to disappear over time just as, despite its early bad reviews, the book became more respectable through the centuries. Fifty years after the invention of the printing press, more than eight million books had been printed. The result was an uncontrolled information glut that eventually resulted in the development of several tools for controlling the information in the book, for establishing relevance, and for instilling a sense of order on the information. These developments included pagination with Arabic numerals, graduated type, indexing, cross-referencing, running heads, tables of contents, and innovations in punctuation marks, paragraphing, and title paging. In constructing useful books, early printers did not follow scribal conventions or previous mental models, but adapted the old manuscript book to the new information technology. The early printers were practical-minded cutting edge technological pioneers who were responding to users' needs and expectations. The book as we know it today arose out of the sweat, mess and grime of the print shop, just as tools for handling Web-based information are emerging from garages, student apartments, and the tiny cubicles of start-up companies.[10]

New information technologies do not usually supplant the old so much as they force the old technologies to take on new roles, just as radio adjusted to television by shifting to talk formats, call-in shows, and the provision of drive-time news and entertainment. In most cases "the old and new technologies coexist and compete for time, attention, money and prestige."[11] This is true in the library where electronic and print-based information are in daily competition for limited resources and for the user's attention. In our daily life newspapers, magazines, radio, and television all compete to bring us the news, with each employing the particular strengths of its medium to the job. In times of change the old technology is always surrounded by institutions "whose organization, not to mention their reason for being, reflects the world view promoted by the technology."[12] Libraries, whose primary technology has been print, and who have served universities whose entire organization is based upon print culture, are lucky that the World Wide Web is currently seen as primarily a print culture that can be viewed on a video monitor. Once it becomes more obvious that the Web is not simply print on a computer screen, but a new medium with its own enabling and transformative powers and effects, both universities and libraries will have had more experience with its effects and will be in a better position to make necessary adjustments. As the long history of man's experience with a succession of information technologies has shown, "society's newly created ways to act often eliminate the very possibility of acting in older ways."[13] While we can do without cars, we are no longer able to easily find stables for our horses; while we can do without CDs, it is increasingly difficult to purchase long-playing records and the equipment to play them on; and while we can do without online catalogs, few libraries have an up-to-date card catalog to which they can return. With the Web will come new ways of acting and the old ways will have to compete for our time and resources.

But technology has to operate within society and so it brings with it a hefty dose of social baggage from the past. Early automobiles still had holders for buggy whips, modern computers still have the old keyboard from manual typewriters, and first-generation online catalogs were often accused of being nothing more than a collection of electronic catalog cards. It has been argued by Joseph Weizenbaum[14] and others that the computer has played an unrecognized conservative role in society. It arrived just in time to avert catastrophic crises and to prevent innovations in banking, welfare, defense, business, and other areas of American society. The computer was a tool that enabled old ways of thought and activity to continue, and allowed society to avoid rethinking procedures and re-examining basic assumptions. Just as computers expanded the number of traditional bank checks, welfare recipients, and catalog cards that could be effectively processed and managed, computers and the Web have opened up the possibility of enabling scholarly communication and higher education to proceed, with minor adjustments, along the old familiar pathways that they have always traveled.

Universities look to the Web with both a mild sense of fear and hope. The fear is because of the emerging social debate about replacing the traditional university with a more electronic version of higher education that would include distance education, a learning-centered environment, and the increasingly centralized control that is possible in a networked world. These buzzwords conceal a change that some faculty and students feel will lead to both a dumbing down and commercialization of education; to a situation in which one Web-based beginning French course will be enough for everyone.[15] But on the other hand, the Web could very well turn out to be the saving grace for the scholarly communication system. The Web may be a tool that enables the present system to avoid a generalized breakdown and to limp along without any substantial changes to its fundamental precepts. The Web provides possibilities by which scholarly communication could be continued without seriously questioning the basic precepts of the 18th century German university research and publication model upon which the current system is based. If the history of information technology is a guide, we can expect that the networked environment and the World Wide Web will cause both scholarly communication and academic libraries to experience some shifting of roles. We can expect the re-structuring of some supporting industries. But there is also a good chance that the more savvy current academic publishers will remain a part of the higher education process, and that libraries will retain their essential mission unchanged. In any case we can be relatively sure that the new communications/information environment will manage to find its own equilibrium either with or without the players who happen to be in the current information chain. As always with technological change, those players who can identify a strong and unambiguous role to fill will survive, and those who can't find such a niche will be in danger of becoming irrelevant.

But librarians are right to be concerned about the ramifications of these changes. The recent history of information technology has seen an increasing amount of information being made available to the masses, instead of being restricted to the elite as it was in the past. Printing, radio, and television all expanded access to information that once was limited to the privileged few, but this information largely flowed in one direction. Each of these technologies put significant obstacles in the way of the lone individual attempting to reach a mass audience. The quantity and quality of communications in these technologies was regulated by gatekeepers who edited and controlled the messages we saw. The Web has removed many of these filters, dramatically lowering the requirements for anyone attempting to reach a mass audience, whether they have anything worthwhile to say or not. Historically, the power of any technology that increases the ability of one central source to directly reach a substantial number of individuals, weakens the power of all the intermediaries in the old information chain. Thus, for example, the printing press provided a way to bypass the authority of the Catholic Church, which in turn led to the Reformation and the beginnings of Protestantism. In a similar way the Web allows anyone to potentially reach an audience of millions, while weakening the intermediary filters and gateways.

This is a disturbing trend for libraries which previously served as one of a limited number of gateways to general information. The Web changes this pre-existing arrangement and allows for the vending of significant information compilations directly to consumers by organizations which are not libraries. In the jargon of the day, libraries have to worry about the potential disintermediation of libraries from the information chain, and the reintermediation of information by large commercial conglomerates with the power to sell complete online libraries to both institutions such as corporations or colleges, and directly to individual consumers. The Web, with its ability to provide the individual with potentially unlimited information for free, including the practical "library of life" information that it now contains, is already a noticeably concrete threat to those of us in the old information chain. By its very nature the Web gives people free access to those subjects that are of the highest interest to the highest numbers of people. The typical gatekeeper's argument that "we know better" is effectively reduced to an echo in an empty room when consumers have the ability to vote with their mouse clicks and money. The only option for information gatekeepers who want to stay relevant is to supply specialized information of undeniable added value. Superior service alone will not make a difference. Milkmen and gas station attendants provided both good service and convenience, and both occupations disappeared in a single generation.

But we've all heard this kind of scare talk before. The future usually turns out to look much like the past. Most of us do not drive helicopters or jet-powered hovercraft to work as earlier predictions said we would be doing in the 1990s. Why is it that the best laid plans don't always turn out as expected? More often than not, it is because human beings are a significant part of the equation and they make up their own quirky minds in their own way. When thinking about the future of collection development and libraries, it is useful to revisit the 3,000-year-old insights of Socrates discussed earlier. Socrates believed that the real time experience of the oral tradition was more conducive to learning than was the solitary reflection of the book. Modern-day thinkers have expanded these insights and given them a slight twist. One of the ways this distinction is discussed today is as two different kinds of cognition: experiential and reflective.

Experiential cognition is the automatic reflexive thought that occurs when a pilot flies a plane, when an athlete makes a split second decision, or when a surgeon encounters the unexpected in the operating room. Experiential cognition occurs in rich dynamic environments and is event driven. Manifestations of this type of cognition occur in arcade games, television, and data processing. Modern Americans experience these cognitive environments through our entertainments such as movies, plays, games, sports, etc., or through interactions with experts who have extensive internalized knowledge in their fields such as mechanics, doctors, and computer specialists.

Reflective cognition, on the other hand, requires quiet and minimal distraction. It is slow and laborious cognition and requires external aids such as writing, books, and people. It requires the ability to store results and to make inferences from stored results. It is the source of new ideas, new concepts and advances in human understanding. It is the realm of problem solving and of following chains of reasoning backwards and forwards. It requires access to the thoughts of others.[16]

The different information needs of experiential and reflective cognition open up several potential pathways for collection development in the emerging information environment. But, meanwhile, libraries are swamped with an excess of information trivia from which to choose and, floundering a bit, uncertain how we should adapt our roles to fit these changing conditions. Vendors offer new products daily, all based upon attempts to sustain the old models and the old players at an ever higher cost; but libraries have been bled dry and no longer have the economic power to prop up these old ways of doing business. In all of this fog are there any harbors that we can make for? Are there any clear directions for libraries to pursue?

There may be three.

The first is books. The Web is not a tool for sustained reading or reflective thought. Libraries and books have been synonymous for thousands of years. Every opinion maker, every educated individual, every school child in the country has used a library and understands the relationship between books and libraries. The library is a place where the tools of reflection and sustained thought may be found. Books are our business whether the words appear on papyrus rolls, are inscribed on parchment, printed on paper, or materialize on the new prototypes of electric paper. And as archivists and technologists tell us, books are a comparatively stable medium that requires neither hardware nor software to decode. Books, orderly sustained thought, and libraries, are a powerful traditional partnership that libraries should strive to continue no matter what future multi-media or networked distractions might arise.

The second harbor for libraries is the Web. The Web today is largely an experiential medium–a tool for advertising, news, games, pinups, gossip, and short bite-sized bits of information. It is a perfect medium for utility information, for information needed to complete a task; and for short consumable items that do not require sustained thought and attention such as journal articles. The Web is a way for libraries to reach users at their desks with short up-to-date utility information such as libraries used to provide through encyclopedias, almanacs, and directories. It is good for items that require a limited amount of time and reflection, such as news and periodical articles. There is a great deal of this type of information already on the Web for free. Libraries cannot compete with the wide scope and low cost of this information, but they can incorporate it and expand upon it by adding value and by purchasing additional practical information to place at their user's fingertips. Information that has been filtered and selected for accuracy by a library or other group will always have added value over information that has not. The Web is also likely to make it more practical for libraries to collect experiential information products such as audio, video, and multi-media. We have been careful about collecting this type of information in the past, but the Web helps to remove some of the practical and philosophical (though not legal) barriers to collecting certain categories of this type of information.

The third role that is emerging for libraries is a redefinition of our role as information middlemen. We simply have to be more demanding and to expect more from our vendors. If we are to continue to occupy a role between vendors and consumers, then we need to add value to the information as it moves through this chain. Added value does not come from passively relaying the information we receive from producers on to the consumer. The added value comes from insisting on quality products at reasonable prices, and from value added by the library's own organizing, linking, retrieval and access systems. Libraries do not exist to insure that an information vendor can jury-rig a new facade on an old business model, charge more money, and continue on their merry way. Some of the vendors we are currently doing business with are not going to make it in this new environment. The new technologies theoretically allow us to exercise more control over cost, yet how many libraries have ever been approached by a publisher or information vendor with a proposal that would help them lower costs? Such proposals are not uncommon in other lines of business. Shouldn't we expect library information vendors to respond to our well-publicized economic needs and to routinely approach us with proposals to help us cut costs?

Jonathan Swift noted three hundred years ago that "vision is the art of seeing things invisible."[17] Libraries, publishers and vendors are all in a changed set of circumstances in which it is important to realize that there are many different ways of making ideas visible. Ideas can be made visible on clay or on papyrus, they can be made visible in our minds through radio, or through our fingertips through Braille. They can be brought to us by stone masons and their chisels, by scribes and reed brushes working on papyrus, and by many different communications media and by many different business models.

Of course, for rock bottom reliable library advice, it is always best to turn to that 16th century library management manual, Machiavelli's *The Prince*. His advice on these matters is simply: "Be lavish only with other people's money. . . . Nothing hurts you except to spend your own money."[18] He also adds cautionary advice on change, saying that "Men gladly change their ruler, believing that they will better themselves. Later they learn through experience that they have become worse off."[19] This could be interpreted as a warning not to throw the books out with the proverbial bathwater. As information becomes available from more sources in more formats, and as the traditional information hierarchies undergo disintermediation and redefinition of their roles, it would not be unexpected if libraries lost some of their relevance and authority. This does not have to be a bad thing. As long as the role libraries choose to play is clear and well defined, then it is not beyond the realm of possibility that in the long run libraries will grow in relevance rather than decline. Unlike other segments of the information chain, the role libraries currently play as a social and institutional cost center for information distribution, allows us to a certain extent to determine what role we want to play in the future. To maintain this role as an information cost center, all we have to do is what we've done for thousands of years: respond to changing conditions, and keep our users satisfied.

In ancient Sparta, when Lycergus did not like the effect the march of civilization was having on his city, he switched the monetary system from gold to iron. Sparta's trading partners did not particularly want iron money so trade ceased. The wealthy found that they had to cart hundreds of pounds of iron money about, and so the advantages of wealth soon disappeared.[20] With this one simple move Lycergus was able to stem the winds of change that had been affecting his city. While I am not suggesting that libraries attempt to pay vendors with iron money, I am saying that Lycergus did change the role that money played in Sparta's economic transactions. This is a good time to repeat the observation that universities possess many kinds of wealth besides cash. Universities have not utilized this wealth to change the current business model in scholarly communication, but there are ways in which they could do so, whether it's as simple as the American Association of Universities proposal to separate peer review from publishing, or other more drastic methods. Options do exist and neither universities nor libraries are helpless pawns in the current system. The bottom line is that the business models our vendors use are something over which we have a certain amount of influence. Periods of change and confusion are always rife with opportunity for the enterprising businessman. It is in these times of turmoil that it becomes even more important for libraries to hold onto core values. When any library agrees to a compromising license or unrealistic price, it sets a precedent that harms both libraries and library users across the land. If vendors are not meeting our needs at a reasonable cost, we need to seek alternatives, or we have no one to blame but ourselves.

In the beginning of this paper there were questions about library vision and focus, our expectations of vendors, and whether electronic information was worth the investment. The principle arguments of the paper are that libraries should be prepared for a redefinition of their role, that they need to stay focused on their primary mission and values, that they will have to be more pro-active and demanding of vendors, and that the world of electronic information is one we should embrace, but with both eyes open and one hand free. It is also important to realize that different information technologies are better suited to different types of cognition and that libraries need to be clear-headed and realistic when they make long-range decisions. Librarians possess a rare combination of skills and experience that is not widely shared among today's information providers. They have a more balanced view of the pluses and minuses of both print and electronic formats than do other players in the arena. If we are to stand up for traditional core library values in regards to electronic information, then now is the time to do it. As Vaclav Havel said recently about the changes in Eastern Europe, "Our main enemy today is our own worst nature: our indifference to the common good."[21] Libraries have been here for thousands of years. We'll be here long after the publishers and businesses we are currently doing business with have merged, split, been absorbed, and quietly disappeared from the face of the earth. As long as we stick to our core mission and do it well, we will be able to weather any information technology that comes along.

It has been said that poets are the priests of the invisible. The opening image in this paper is that of a poet who utilizes the hawks to make visible the winds blowing in off the Pacific. Librarians don't want only to make visible the myriad ideas of human thought, they want to sift through these thoughts and collect the best. To do this they weave nets in which to catch these metaphorical winds and the ideas they contain. Of course, weaving nets to catch the wind is a good working definition of a completely hopeless, idealistic and impractical occupation. Except we need to remember that nets made to catch the wind are called sails. And sails are one of man's great technological innovations. So that is the thought I'll leave you with: Librarians weaving nets to catch the wind, librarians as the fishermen of human thought. Librarians doing the job they have always done.

REFERENCES

1. Kurt Andersen, "The Digital Bubble," New Yorker (Jan 19, 1998), 30.

2. "Networked Information: Finding what's Out There, an interview with Clifford Lynch," Educom Review (November/December 1997), 42-50.

3. Seneca, Epistulae Morales, no.71, section 3.

4. Donald A. Norman. Things that make us smart: defending human attributes in the age of the machine (Reading, MA: Addison-Wesley Pub. Co., c1993), 44.

5. Neil Postman, Technopoly: the surrender of culture to technology (New York: Knopf, 1992), 4.

6. Neil Postman, Amusing ourselves to death: public discourse in the age of show business (New York: Viking, 1985), 252.

7. Bible. Old Testament, Daniel, chapter 12, verse 4.

8. Dan Lacy, From Grunts to Gigabytes (Urbana: University of Illinois Press, 1996), 153.

9. Communication in History: technology, culture, society, edited by David Crowley & Paul Heyer (White Plains, NY: Longman Publishers, 1995), 30.

10. Elizabeth Eisenstein, The Printing Press as an Agent of Change (Cambridge: Cambridge University Press, 1979).

11. Neil Postman, Technopoly: the surrender of culture to technology (New York: Knopf, 1992), 16.

12. Neil Postman, Technopoly: the surrender of culture to technology (New York: Knopf, 1992), 18.

13. Joseph Weisenbaum "Computers, Tools, and Human Reason," Communication in History: technology, culture, society, edited by David Crowley & Paul Heyer (White Plains, NY: Longman Publishers, 1995), 282.

14. Joseph Weisenbaum "Computers, Tools, and Human Reason," Communication in History: technology, culture, society, edited by David Crowley & Paul Heyer (White Plains, NY: Longman Publishers, 1995).

15. David Noble, "Digital Diploma Mills: The Automation of Higher Education," First Monday: Peer Reviewed Journal on the Internet (Vol.3 No.1 - January 5th. 1998). URL: http: //www.firstmonday.dk/issues/issue3_1/noble/index.html

16. Donald A. Norman. Things that make us smart: defending human attributes in the age of the machine (Reading, Mass.: Addison-Wesley Pub. Co., c1993), 24-34.

17. Jonathan Swift, "Thoughts on Various Subjects," quoted in The Home Book of Quotations, Burton Stevenson, editor (New York: Dodd, Mead, 1967).

18. Niccolo Machiavelli, "The Prince," Selections. English. 1965 The Chief works, and Others. Translated by Allan Gilbert (Durham, NC, Duke University Press, 1965), chapter 6.

19. Niccolo Machiavelli, "The Prince," Selections. English. 1965 The Chief works, and Others. Translated by Allan Gilbert (Durham, NC, Duke University Press, 1965), chapter 3.

20. Plutarch, Lives from Plutarch. The modern American ed. of twelve lives edited and abridged, with an introd. by John W. McFarland (New York, Random House, 1967).

21. Vaclav Havel, The Art of the Impossible: Politics as Morality in Practice: speeches and writings, 1990-1996 (New York, Knopf, 1997), 8.

Building the Global Collection–
World Class Collection Development:
A Chronicle of the AAU/ARL
Global Resources Program

Mary Case
Deborah Jakubs

When *Time* Magazine honored Dr. David Ho as its Man of the Year in December 1996,[1] it chronicled the work not only of a single individual, but of many scientists from around the world who have contributed to the advancement of the understanding of AIDS. Scientists from Paris, Antwerp, Bethesda, San Francisco, Durham, from research centers, universities, and industry, have all played a role in piecing together the causes of and treatments for one of this century's most devastating epidemics.

When the Asian stock markets crashed several months ago, the ramifications were felt around the globe. Stock markets closed, banks failed, companies folded. International bailouts were necessary to prevent worldwide disaster.

Closer to home, the library community was thrust into the international scene when the World Intellectual Property Organization (WIPO) took

Mary Case is Director of the Office of Scholarly Communication at The Association of Research Libraries in Washington, DC.

Deborah Jakubs is Director of Collection Services at Duke University in Durham, NC.

[Haworth co-indexing entry note]: "Building the Global Collection–World Class Collection Development: A Chronicle of the AAU/ARL Global Resources Program." Case, Mary, and Deborah Jakubs. Co-published simultaneously in *Journal of Library Administration* (The Haworth Information Press, an imprint of The Haworth Press, Inc.) Vol. 28, No. 1, 1999, pp. 63-80; and: *Collection Development in a Digital Environment* (ed: Sul H. Lee) The Haworth Information Press, an imprint of The Haworth Press, Inc., 1999, pp. 63-80. Single or multiple copies of this article are available for a fee from The Haworth Document Delivery Service [1-800-342-9678, 9:00 a.m. - 5:00 p.m. (EST). E-mail address: getinfo@haworthpressinc.com].

63

up the cause of copyright in the digital age at its meetings in Brussels in December 1996. As a result of the U.S. delegation of librarians and educators, the concept of fair use was embraced by WIPO and the most potentially damaging of WIPO proposals were defeated or tabled.

These events and many others over the past decade have made it very clear that we are in an age where our fate is intricately linked to that of other nations. Research is international, the economy global, and public policy is now fashioned by world-wide treaties. As Rosabeth Moss Kanter notes in her 1995 work, *World Class: Thriving Locally in the Global Economy,* the force of globalization is "one of the most powerful and pervasive influences on nations, businesses, workplaces, communities, and lives at the end of the twentieth century."[2]

It is ironic that during this time when the notion of the global economy is strong and universities are encouraging the internationalization of their research programs and curricula, support for international resources in the research libraries of this country has severely eroded. In 1996, the Association of Research Libraries (ARL) published a report documenting both the decline in the acquisitions of foreign language materials in research library collections and the increase in the homogeneity of these collections.[3] This four-year study of trends in global information resources funded by The Andrew W. Mellon Foundation found that the increasing volume of publishing output around the world, the dramatic fluctuations in exchange rates, the steadily rising prices of science, technology, and medical journals, and the emergence of new electronic resources have all combined to put enormous pressure on library collections budgets. The report notes that one of the first responses to this pressure has been to cut back on the purchase of low-use foreign language materials. With individual libraries making this same decision simultaneously–concentrating on the acquisition of English language materials in core disciplines–the research library collections of this country have become less comprehensive and more alike. Thinking locally has undermined the library community's ability to support the information needs of the emerging global economy.

Concerned about these trends, the Association of American Universities (AAU) created in 1993 a Task Force on the Acquisition and Distribution of Foreign Language and Area Studies Materials. The final report of the Task Force, issued in April 1994, recommended the creation of a "networked-based, distributed program for the development of foreign acquisitions for U.S. and Canadian research libraries."[4] The Task Force also recommended the creation of three pilot projects to help better understand the challenges presented by distributed access and the effects of such a system on the users of area studies collections. Research materials from Latin America, Germany, and Japan were targeted.

Building on these recommendations, the Association of Research Libraries developed a *Strategic Plan for Improving Access to Global Information Resources in U.S. and Canadian Research Libraries.*[5] Endorsed by the ARL Board of Directors in July of 1995, the plan called for the development of "a seamless web of interconnected, coordinated, and interdependent research collections that are electronically accessible to geographically distributed users."[6] The three pilot projects proposed by the AAU Task Force would serve as the start-up phase of an effort whose ultimate goal was to create a world-wide program. The subsequent tactical plan formed the basis of a $450,000 proposal to The Mellon Foundation to scale up the three demonstration projects to create a Global Resources Program. Mellon approved the funding request in December 1996 and Deborah Jakubs, Head, International and Area Studies, Duke University Libraries, was named Program Director.

The ARL report noted that the success of a cooperative Global Resources Program would depend on the ability of the library and university community to effect "a fundamental shift in the culture or the expectations of faculty, students, and scholars."[7] In the concepts of Kanter, it is in part a shift in mindset from the "local" to the "cosmopolitan." According to Kanter, cosmopolitans are "card-carrying members of the world class" who "possess portable skills and a broad outlook." Cosmopolitans "bring the best and latest concepts, the highest levels of competence, and excellent connections. . . ."[8] Their broad vision and access to global resources, however, is intimately connected with a "responsiveness to the needs of the communities in which they operate."[9] A world class organization nurtures cosmopolitans both to build global networks and to enrich the local environment. How do we bring about the shifts in outlook, skills, and infrastructure necessary to support a network of world class libraries and library collections?

GENERAL LIBRARY TRENDS

Librarians are now very familiar with the trends that have so affected library collections budgets and purchasing patterns over the past two decades. Against the backdrop of increasing worldwide production of books and journals have come increasing prices and fluctuations in currencies. According to statistics gathered by UNESCO (generally acknowledged to under-report given the difficulty of gathering reliable data in many Third World countries), "international book output increased from 715,500 titles in 1980 to just below the one million mark in 1992,"[10] or approximately 28%. Between 1980 and 1990, book production in developed countries increased from 562,500 to 600,000 titles (only 7%), while that in third world countries increased from 153,000 to 242,000 titles (or 58%). While the U.S. proportion of international output declined slightly from 13.8% to 12.6% over the same period, the proportion of Asian countries' production rose from 18.8% to 26.7%. China is now the world's most prolific publisher with almost 101,000 titles produced in 1994. U.S. book production reached an all-time high in 1995 of 62,039 titles.[11] As a point of comparison, the typical ARL library purchased 26,262 monographs in 1996.[12]

Publication of journals has also risen dramatically since 1980. *Ulrich's International Periodicals Directory* listed 96,000 titles in 1980/81 and 165,000 in 1996 (an increase of 72%).[13] In 1996, the typical ARL library subscribed to 15,069 serial titles.[14]

This increase in numbers, however, has also been accompanied in some subject areas by significant increases in prices. Journals in science, technology, and medicine (stm) are both higher in price and increasing in price faster than journals in most other fields. According to the 1997 "Periodicals Price Survey," published in *Library Journal*,[15] the average price for a title in physics is almost $1500; chemistry, $1360; math, $818; biology, $824; and health sciences, $543. Compare these to titles in the humanities, such as history, $96; language and literature, $90; philosophy and religion, $113; and art, $108. According to the "Latin American Periodical Price Index," the average Latin American book was $79 in 1996/97.[16] Between 1986 and 1996, statistics gathered by ARL show an average unit cost of serials subscribed to by a typical research library increasing from $88.81 to $219.46.[17]

Also dramatic is the rate of price increases of the stm titles. Between 1993 and 1997, physics journals increased in price by over 50%, biology almost 54%, chemistry over 45%, math over 55%, and health sciences almost 53%. In contrast, history titles increased by 32%, language by 33%, philosophy and religion by 31%, and art by 18%. ARL statistics indicate that the average annual subscription cost has increased by 9.5% a year between 1986 and 1996.[18]

While less dramatic, the prices of books have also increased over the past decade and a half. The average North American scholarly monograph cost $25 in 1981 and $48.11 in 1995 (an increase of 92%).[19] In 1987, the average academic book in the UK cost 23.81 pounds, and in 1993, it cost 35.39 pounds, an increase of 48.6%. In Spain, the increase in price over the same period for all books was 80.9%, for Italy, 29.8%, Japan, 24.5%, and Brazil, 1.2%.[20] ARL data records an increase of 5% a year in the cost of monographs between 1986 and 1996, from $28.65 to $46.73.[21]

Exacerbating the rising prices of all library materials have been the fluctuations in the value of the dollar against foreign currencies. Beginning in late 1985 and continuing until 1990, the U.S. and Canadian currencies lost significant value against most of the currencies of the major trading nations. The dollar regained some strength in the early 1990s, declined in 1994, and is now gaining strength again.

A stark representation of the effects of these trends can be seen in Figure 1 representing monograph and serial costs in ARL libraries from 1986 to 1996.[22] The precipitous drop in monograph purchases between 1986 and 1987 parallels the significant declines in the value of the dollar. The initial response of individual libraries to large increases in foreign subscription prices was to buy fewer monographs until serial cancellation projects could be undertaken. Moreover, with the continuing increase in volume and price of both journals and monographs and continued fluctuations in currency, libraries have been unable to regain the buying power that they had in 1986. In fact, the typical research library purchased 21% fewer monographs in 1996 than it did in 1986 while spending 29% more, and purchased 7% fewer serial subscriptions while spending 124% more.

EFFECT OF TRENDS ON AREA STUDIES

Especially vulnerable during this sustained period of financial pressure have been the foreign language/area studies collections. Foreign

FIGURE 1. Monograph and Serial Costs in ARL Libraries, 1986-1997

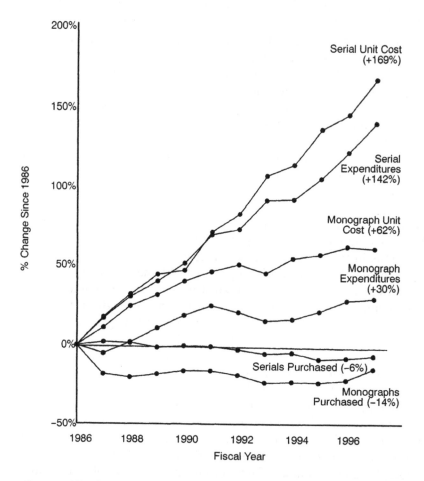

Source: *ARL Statistics 1996-97,* Association of Research Libraries, Washington, DC.

language titles are frequently low-use materials, hence, easier targets during budget cutbacks. Contributing to the low use are the decline in foreign language requirements in several disciplines and the lack of coverage by indexing and abstracting services.[23] Area studies budgets can also be pressured by 'taxes' for electronic resources. Since area studies electronic products tend to be high cost and low use, they are not likely candidates for centralized funding. In this case, area studies loses both in the opportunity to have electronic resources purchased and in the tax on its budget to support electronic products in other disciplines.

Evidence of the vulnerability of these materials can be found in an analysis of foreign non-serial titles with imprint dates of 1988 through 1994 found in the OCLC database in March 1995. For 1988, the OCLC database included 290,531 unique titles from nine regions of the world cataloged by North American OCLC member libraries. For 1994, there were 222,921 unique titles, a decrease of 23%. In addition, "the greatest number of overseas monographs published between 1988 and 1994 and acquired by North American libraries were in English, followed by French and German."[24]

These patterns were corroborated in a study conducted by Anna Perrault for her doctoral dissertation.[25] Perrault analyzed the collecting behavior of 72 ARL libraries between 1985 and 1989. The analysis found that "there was a steep decline in foreign language acquisitions, a decrease in the percentage of unique titles in many subject areas, and an increased concentration on core materials. The overall decline in the rate of monographic acquisitions from 1985 to 1989 for the group was 27.76 percent" (from 144,879 unique titles in 1985 to 104,660 titles in 1989). "Foreign language imprints experienced a much greater decline than English language imprints." From virtually the same base, English imprints decreased by 12.34%, while non-English imprints decreased by 43.33%. "The analysis by specific subject areas indicates that the group of 72 ARL libraries selected more titles in common in 1989 than in 1985, resulting in a greater concentration of core titles in central disciplines."

During these two decades of declining resources, area studies librarians were faced with yet another dilemma. Universities–understanding the importance of international interdependence–encouraged faculty to internationalize their research programs and curricula. This new emphasis put additional pressure on area studies programs to broaden their collections beyond the traditional disciplines of language, literature, art, religion, and philosophy, to include such fields as economic development, environmental studies, demographics, and interdisciplinary studies. The need to extend already eroding resources to a broader array of disciplines has resulted in both a decrease of the overall purchase of foreign resources and a narrowing of the scope across disciplines to core titles only. By responding locally to these significant pressures, libraries have eroded their ability to sustain a world class global information resource.

Libraries know what the alternative to responding locally is, and have in fact engaged in numerous cooperative collection development efforts over the years. These efforts, however, often wither in times of budget pressure when libraries must respond to local priorities. While certainly understandable, no cooperative collection development program can be considered successful unless its commitments are sustained during difficult financial times.

The ARL Foreign Acquisitions Project acknowledged the difficulty of cooperation, but also recognized that the rise of new information technologies afforded "an unprecedented opportunity to rethink the ways research libraries manage global resources and to fashion cooperative strategies for ensuring the success of the aggregate holdings."[26] Technology can facilitate the identification and location of resources held around the globe, and as more and more resources are digitized, it can ease the delivery of text, data, and images. It can also speed communication among an international array of users, libraries, and suppliers. But technology will not solve all of the problems. Libraries still need to deal with vast stores of print material that will require improvements in interlibrary loan services. In addition, there are coordination problems, technology access impediments, human resource, and political issues. But as ARL and AAU concluded, it was time to seriously confront and address these challenges.

AAU/ARL GLOBAL RESOURCES PROGRAM[27]

The primary goal of the Global Resources Program is "to improve access to international research resources and to help libraries contain costs, especially through the establishment of models of distributed collecting and the use of technology."[28] The program's initial efforts have focused on collaborative projects to obtain access to research materials in Latin America, Japan, and Germany. Additional projects on Africa, South Asia, and Southeast Asia are under development.

The three original projects were selected because each area had been identified in the ARL Foreign Acquisitions Project as needing attention. Each had also been successful in attracting external funding, was an area of current interest in national collaborative efforts, and presented a different level of electronic capacity.

The Latin American project was intended to focus on serials, government documents, and working papers and technical reports from non-governmental organizations. Key to its selection was the work of the Seminar on the Acquisition of Latin American Library Materials (SALALM), an active organization in the field with a successful record for supporting cooperative collection development efforts. Also of note was the expressed interest of The Mellon Foundation in funding the development of a network between North and South American research libraries to provide access to Latin American resources. In addition, electronic resources were just beginning to become available in Latin America.

Cooperative collecting in the traditional area studies disciplines was already strong for Japanese resources. A new project focusing on recent interest in Japanese scientific and technical research could, therefore, build on the supporting organizational and networked infrastructure developed by the National Coordinating Committee for Japanese Libraries. This project would focus on Japanese language journals in high-impact science fields. By concentrating on a different subject area, this project could potentially attract new sources of funding.

In the case of Germany, the demonstration project would seek to enrich access to social science resources in all languages published in Germany. Western European programs are strong, with many faculty and considerable collections. The bibliographic and acquisitions infrastructure is well-developed as is the infrastructure for information technology; but library resources are expensive.

Planning for all three projects began in 1994, but progress has been variable. With a project coordinator, two major grants from The Mellon Foundation, and a commitment of participating member staff and financial resources, the Latin American project has made great strides. The Japan project has a part-time coordinator supported by OCLC and has received funds for the project server. No funds, however, have been available for support services, such as loading the project journal files. Until recently, when the German project received the assistance of a part-time program coordinator, progress on that project had been slower than desired. Details on the progress of each project are noted below.

Latin America

The most ambitious of the projects thus far has been the Latin Americanist Research Resources Pilot Project. The Latin American project began in 1994 with start-up funding from The Mellon Foundation and contributions from 35 participating ARL libraries. Additional funding from Mellon in October 1995 supported a second phase. The project has focused on improving access to Argentine and Mexican serials, government documents, and the publications of research institutes. Participating libraries, now 39, have divided up subscription responsibility for about 300 serials from Argentina and Mexico. The tables-of-contents of these titles are entered by individual libraries into a database maintained by the University of Texas Latin American Network Information Center (UT-LANIC). Work has begun on expanding the table-of-contents to include data back to 1990. Libraries have also agreed to support the delivery of articles via Interlibrary Loan. User-initiated ILL is provided for the titles in the project through OCLC. Recently, participating libraries were asked to cancel one project title for which they do not have responsibility and assume responsibility for a new title, thus expanding the database.

A second aspect of the Latin American project is the digitization of presidential messages from Argentina and Mexico. The scanning and indexing of the documents is nearly complete.

The collection of non-governmental organizations'(NGOs) working papers and technical reports has proven to be more problematic than anticipated. The NGOs are numerous and acquiring their publications turned out to be extremely staff-intensive. The Project Working Group on NGOs is in the process of rethinking the acquisitions strategy for these materials.

In 1997, a monographic component was added to the project. Participating libraries agree to reallocate either $3,000 or 7% of their Latin American monographic budgets to deepen coverage in an area in which they already have a strong collection. This strategy strengthens local collections while expanding the national resource base and encouraging interdependence among libraries. Thus far, the participating libraries have reallocated $152,000 to deepening their collections. This is about the cost of creating one new Latin American research collection.

One of the most important developments of the Latin American work is the structure that has been put in place to manage the project. The participating institutions created six Working Groups and an Advisory Committee to coordinate the project. Working Group members, librarians in the participating institutions, are volunteers who are also members of SALALM and meet in conjunction with SALALM meetings. With this structure, the work becomes institutionalized, rather than left to a central coordinator.

Japan

The Japanese Journals Access Project began in earnest in early 1997 with a call for participation. Twenty-eight ARL libraries responded and are now working with the National Coordinating Committee on Japanese Library Resources on a broader charge to increase access to all Japanese journal literature, not just science and technology journals. The Project's goals are to improve access to Japanese journals available in both North America and Japan. To improve access to journals in North America, project participants plan to develop a Web-based union list, a collaborative collection development program, links from the union list Website to document supply services, and a funding proposal for retrospective conversion of Japanese serial files. To improve access to Japanese held journals, the project participants hope to gain access to standard Japanese bibliographic sources now available electronically and to develop relationships with Japanese libraries and other organizations to sort out issues related to interlibrary loan, such as copyright and currency exchange.

Progress thus far includes the performance of feasibility tests for loading records from participants' online catalogs into the Web-based union list. The project Website has been updated to include links to sites of potential value for locating serials and enabling document delivery.[29] Contacts have been made with ARL counterpart libraries in Japan and negotiations are underway to work through issues to ease interlibrary loan with Japanese libraries. In addition, the National Center for Science Information Systems (NACSIS) is making available indefinitely and at no cost its Webcat, which contains both the Union List of Books and the Union List of Serials for over 400 Japanese libraries.

Germany

Twenty-two libraries have committed to participating in the German Demonstration Project. The project's primary goals are (1) to ensure effective and timely access to German language research materials through electronic resource sharing and improved interlibrary document delivery services; and (2) to test linking between North American and German libraries to expand access to specialized research resources.

This project has been somewhat slowed in its development due to lack of funding and dedicated staff. Several recent developments should, however, lead to significant progress in 1998. The American Institute of Contemporary German Studies of Johns Hopkins University has generously offered the services of a part-time project coordinator. In addition, The Mellon Foundation has just provided a special grant to the Global Resources Program to fund a preliminary meeting in the United States in June and a subsequent conference in Germany involving German and North American librarians. The grant will also support the crafting of American and German digital collection development agreements, improved document delivery, and a report on ways to improve access to German digital material and Internet publications. The recent development of a German document delivery system with a link for North American libraries should also begin to provide the infrastructure for facilitating interlibrary loan between Germany and North America.

NEW AREA PROJECTS

South Asia

The "Digital South Asia Library: A Pilot Project" is the first new project of the Global Resources Program. Led by the University of Chicago Library and Columbia University Libraries, in collaboration with two libraries in India,[30] the two-year project seeks to create new electronic reference resources and to build the infrastructure for intercontinental document delivery to and from selected South Asian libraries. Major outcomes expected of the project include electronic indexing records for Tamil, Urdu, and English journal articles published during the 19th and 20th centuries; electronic full-text versions of classic 19th-century South Asia reference books printed in roman characters; full-text electronic versions of titles from the Official Publications of India; and delivery on demand of page images via the Internet of the Tamil and Urdu journal articles indexed under this project. This project was approved for a Global Resources start-up grant in late 1997.

Africa

The Africana Librarians Council of the African Studies Association (ALC/ASA) and the Cooperative Africana Microform Project (CAMP) of the Center for Research Libraries (CRL) have proposed to develop a Web-based union list of African newspapers. The project would focus on newspapers of sub-Saharan Africa regardless of date or language. It would start with holdings in the United States and be expanded to include holdings in Africa. CRL has offered to host the project. This project proposal is currently undergoing final drafting.

Southeast Asia

The Committee on Research Materials on Southeast Asia (COR-MOSEA) librarians are also in the process of drafting a final proposal. They will seek funding to support the creation of a distributed index to Southeast Asian vernacular journal literature. The project will be divided into two components: (1) the conversion of existing indexing databases to a common format that will be loaded to a central server; and (2) the development of mechanisms for management and retrieval of vernacular journal texts.

OTHER ACTIVITIES IN SUPPORT OF ACCESS TO FOREIGN RESOURCES

In addition to area projects, the Global Resources Program has also begun to undertake other activities in support of access to foreign resources. These include the development of a clearinghouse of Web-sites that support international research, organized by region and country.[31] As a part of this effort, area studies specialists were asked to identify sites to be included. The Program Director has also surveyed ARL libraries to identify the formal and informal linkages that may already exist with institutions abroad. Such linkages could form the basis of new projects or expand participation in current ones. Similarly, to build on current efforts, the Program Director has had discussions with the Center for Research Libraries on the possibility of future collaborative initiatives, as well as preliminary discussions with the Library of Congress, the Research Libraries Group (RLG), OCLC, the American Council of Learned Societies (ACLS), and the Committee on Interinstitutional Cooperation (CIC). Initiatives are also underway on the training of area librarians, including a workshop on area librarianship at Duke University in spring 1998.

Of critical importance to the goals of the Global Resources Program is the engagement of faculty on the key issues surrounding cooperative collection development and distributed access. Conversations are underway with the ACLS to explore opportunities for ARL and ACLS to collaborate in areas related to the Global Resources Program. One possible effort would bring together small groups of scholars and librarians to develop a set of strategic initiatives for each world area, as well as for broader international issues.

An important component of the Global Resources Program is its Advisory Board. Made up of faculty, senior administrators, and librarians, the Advisory Board is the key link to the AAU and is intended to champion the priorities of the Global Resources Program within the academic community.[32]

THE CHALLENGES AHEAD

While much progress is being made, the Global Resources Program faces many challenges as it seeks to build a world-class network of libraries. A very clear lesson derived from the experience of the first three projects is that while the ultimate goal is to integrate the projects into the normal functioning of the participating libraries, initial progress depends to a great extent on start-up funding and the availability of a project coordinator. The cooperative nature of the projects requires a significant amount of coordination, communication, and follow-up that is not easily factored into the day-to-day functioning of the area studies librarian in the current environment. It also helps if the project can be supported within the framework of an existing professional organization. The connection of the Latin American project to SALALM and the Japanese project to the National Coordinating Committee for Japanese Libraries provide regular meeting opportunities and professional relationships that facilitate coordination and communication.

The projects are also revealing that administrative commitment along with the involvement of library colleagues, such as the interlibrary loan librarian and the head of collection development, are often necessary to carry out the cooperative agreements. Many of the benefits of the projects derive from value-added activities that both add to the responsibilities of area studies librarians and include functions that are outside their purview. Again, if the projects are going to be integrated into the normal functioning of the library, colleagues need to be involved in the planning, policy-making, and implementation of a project, particularly as it affects the individual library. Moreover, their willingness to cooperate may be determined by the degree of commitment of the university librarian.

Another lesson from the program has to do with the importance of generating new thinking within libraries if the goals of the Global Resources Program are to be achieved. Reallocation of resources to support the long-term goals of each project has proven more difficult than originally anticipated, since the approaches suggested by the projects may be viewed as experimental, functioning *in addition* to earlier ways of providing access, rather than as replacements for those methods. Thus, for example, libraries are slow to cancel journals and rely on other institutions, just as they are reluctant to draw their collection policies more tightly to play a better defined role in a model of distributed access. The successful implementation of the projects, and of the program in general, will require a shift in thinking about what libraries acquire, why they acquire what they do, and how they make resources accessible. This will require close collaboration between librarians and faculty, as well as a very clear commitment on the part of library directors and staff to the concepts of distributed collections.

While funds from The Mellon Foundation have indeed been generous, additional funds will be needed to help launch new projects. As noted earlier, start-up funding is one of the key factors in the progress made by a project. While participating libraries have been providing some funding in addition to seed money from The Mellon grant, this model will not sustain the long-term financial health of the program. The Advisory Board is currently considering other models. However, without a clearer sense of the benefits of participation and the incentives for those institutions that take the lead, and the demonstration that ARL institutions are actually committed to this approach, it is somewhat difficult to make the case for additional funding.

Yet another important challenge facing the Global Resources Program is the endangered status of area studies librarians. New librarians are not entering this field. As a group, area specialists are older than other librarians, who are, in fact, older than other professions.[33] Over

40% of area librarians are over 50 years old. In addition, as budgets are pressured, area studies librarians have been redeployed, assigned more general responsibilities in the library. At the same time, with the advent of technology and the internationalization of the curriculum, the range of responsibilities for those who retain area studies tasks is increasing. As is true of many others in the library, area studies librarians are now expected to learn new electronic resources and provide training, develop Web pages, participate in grant writing, fund raising, and outreach. But the 'traditional' roles, which require a deep knowledge of selection resources, the book trade, and faculty interests, and an enormous amount of time for selection and the nurturing of important relationships with book dealers, exchange partners, faculty, and students, have not really changed. Moreover, with the Global Resources Projects, area studies librarians are being asked to take on additional tasks related to the development of proposals, writing of interinstitutional agreements, and the implementation and management of these agreements.

The Global Resources Program seeks to reaffirm the importance of area studies librarians at the same time that it seeks to redefine their role. It is also a priority of the program to ensure that there are new librarians entering the field with the appropriate skills and training to carry out the long-term goals of the program. Some models for training have been developed to attract individuals with strong subject backgrounds into librarianship. For example, Duke University offers a Mellon Post-Doctoral Fellowship in Latin American Research Librarianship, and Indiana University offers a joint Master's degree between the library school and area studies programs. Other models such as internships are also needed, however, to increase the visibility of area studies as a legitimate and rewarding career path for librarians.

CONCLUSION

Leaders of world class organizations, according to Kanter, need an understanding of the global environment and a commitment to cosmopolitanism. World class organizations emphasize innovation, learning, and collaboration, and organize around the customer. This suggests that the Global Resources Program, to meet its goal of establishing a world class network of libraries, needs the understanding and commitment of the highest levels of leadership not only in libraries, but also in university administrations. Also required is a central role for the scholars and students who will have access to the vast array of international resources provided by this network. Moreover, collaboration with library and faculty colleagues around the world working together toward innovative solutions is essential.

The Global Resources Program is making significant progress in all of these areas. As can be seen from this chronicle, however, there are still challenges ahead. But the potential benefits of an interconnected world-wide network of research libraries are too great not to confront these obstacles. We should not miss this opportunity to build a "framework for sharing research collections" that will be effective not only for "foreign materials but all other library resources."[34]

NOTES

1. "The Disease Detective," *Time*, Dec. 30, 1996-Jan. 6, 1997, p. 56-73.

2. Rosabeth Moss Kanter, *World Class: Thriving Locally in the Global Economy* (New York: Touchstone, 1997, c1995), 11.

3. Jutta Reed-Scott, *Scholarship, Research Libraries, and Global Publishing* (Washington, D.C.: Association of Research Libraries, 1996).

4. "Report of the AAU Task Force on Acquisition and Distribution of Foreign Language and Area Studies Materials," in *Reports of the AAU Task Force* (Washington, D.C.: Association of Research Libraries, May 1995), 1-41.

5. Reed-Scott, 143-151.

6. Ibid., 145.

7. Ibid., 138.

8. Kanter, 22-23.

9. Ibid., 25.

10. Reed-Scott, 29.

11. *Bowker Annual*, 1997 (New Providence, New Jersey: R.R. Bowker), 521.

12. *ARL Statistics: 1995-1996* (Washington, D.C.: Association of Research Libraries, 1997), 9.

13. 1980/81 data from Ann Okerson, "Of making many Books There is No end: Report on Serial Prices for the Association of Research Libraries," in *Report of the ARL Serials Prices Project* (Washington, DC: Association of Research Libraries, 1989), 15; 1996 data from *Ulrichs International Periodicals Directory 1996* (New Providence, N.J.: R.R. Bowker, 1996), vii.

14. *ARL Statistics*: 1995-1996, 9.

15. Lee Ketcham and Kathleen Born, "Unsettled Times, Unsettled Prices: 37th Annual Report, Periodical Price Survey 1997," *Library Journal* 122 (April 15, 1997):42-47.

16. "Latin American Periodical Price Index," *SALALM Newsletter*, v. 25, no. 3 (Dec. 1997), 72.

17. *ARL Statistics: 1995-1996*, 9.

18. Ibid.

19. "North American Academic Books Index," *Bowker Annual* (New Providence, New Jersey: R.R. Bowker), 1986,1991,1997.

20. Reed-Scott, 43.

21. *ARL Statistics: 1995-1996*, 9.

22. Ibid., 8.

23. Reed-Scott, 52-53.

24. Ibid., 59.

25. Anna H. Perrault, "Study Confirms Increased Homogeneity in Academic Library Acquisitions," *ARL* 180 (May 1995):5.

26. Reed-Scott, xix.

27. Information on recent developments in the program has been taken from: *AAU/ARL Global Resources Program: Status Report*, April 1997 and September 1997; and *The AAU/ARL Global Resources Program: A Report to The Andrew W. Mellon Foundation from the Association of Research Libraries on the First year of the Grant (No. 49600636) January - December 1997*, February 1998.

28. *AAU/ARL Global Resources Program: Status Report* September 1997, p. 1.

29. http://pears.lib.ohio-state.edu

30. The Roja Muthiah Research Library (Madras) and the Sundarayya Vignana Kendram (Hyderabad).

31. http://www.duke.edu/~frykholm/global3.htm

32. Members of the Board include: Betty Bengtson, Director of University Libraries, University of Washington and Chair of the Advisory Board; Myles Brand, President, Indiana University; John D'Arms, President, American Council of Learned Societies; Joe Hewitt, Chair of the ARL Research Collections Committee, *ex officio*; Deborah Jakubs (ARL), Head, International and Area Studies, Duke University Libraries; Stanley Katz, Professor, Princeton University; Hwa-Wei Lee, Dean of University Libraries, Ohio University; Carole Moore, Chief Librarian, University of Toronto; Suzanne Thorin, University Librarian, Indiana University; John Vaughn, Executive Vice President, Association of American Universities, *ex officio*; and David Wiley, Professor, Michigan State University, and Co-Chair, Council of National Resource Center Directors.

33. Stanley J. Wilder, *Age Demographics of Academic Librarians: A Profession Apart* (Washington, D.C.: Association of Research Libraries, 1995), 51.

34. Reed-Scott, 127.

Scenario Planning
and Collection Development

Joan Giesecke

Most of the press these days on the world of information seems to believe that we are all building virtual libraries for virtual students of the virtual university. Reports on the demise of higher education as we know it abound and the latest hope for the future is distance education efforts. Financing higher education is an ongoing crisis with many elected and appointed boards and officials beginning to believe that all will be saved by a telecommunications structure that will somehow free them from having to support higher education. They also believe that somehow information will be free–or as the popular saying goes–Everything you need is on the Internet and it's free. Even the Rand Corporation's Council for Aid to Education, in a report entitled "Breaking the Social Contract" implies that content will be free to the user. To quote from their recommendation on libraries, "Substantial savings and improved library services can be obtained by focusing on the software needed to place library resources on the Internet rather than continuing to support individual research library collections."[1] One wonders where these "experts" have been lately. Have they ever seen an invoice for an electronic publication? Do they have any idea that Elsevier exists?

But, for us, the question isn't so much what the experts think, but what kind of future do we envision for ourselves? How do we see the

---

Joan Giesecke is Dean of Libraries at the University of Nebraska-Lincoln in Lincoln, NE.

[Haworth co-indexing entry note]: "Scenario Planning and Collection Development." Giesecke, Joan. Co-published simultaneously in *Journal of Library Administration* (The Haworth Information Press, an imprint of The Haworth Press, Inc.) Vol. 28, No. 1, 1999, pp. 81-92; and: *Collection Development in a Digital Environment* (ed: Sul H. Lee) The Haworth Information Press, an imprint of The Haworth Press, Inc., 1999, pp. 81-92. Single or multiple copies of this article are available for a fee from The Haworth Document Delivery Service [1-800-342-9678, 9:00 a.m. - 5:00 p.m. (EST). E-mail address: getinfo@haworthpressinc.com].

library collection developing over the next 5 to 10 years? How can we predict the future and, more importantly, what if we guess wrong?

In changing times with many uncertainties, managers need planning processes that encourage flexibility and creativity. We can think strategically about the future; we can envision an ideal future. But in the practical, real world of decision-making, we need a system that helps us to both think the unthinkable and plan for multiple options. We can not always guess correctly about the future, so we need to design techniques that let us envision a variety of options and then plan for those possibilities.

One technique that can help managers plan for multiple futures is scenario-driven planning. Scenario planning is a structured, disciplined technique for identifying key driving forces in the environment that have an impact on the organization and then using that information to design a series of scenarios or stories that describe possible futures. Using these stories, managers can design strategies that will help the organization reach its goal under a variety of circumstances. The stories help managers identify their own assumptions about the future and test those assumptions as they review and renew the scenarios.

The result of scenario planning exercise is not an accurate prediction of the future. Rather, the stories provide managers with options to consider and help managers create their own futures. Managers can make better decisions when they have considered, discussed, and imagined a variety of options and not just worst case, best case scenarios.

The classic scenario-driven planning experience is that of the Royal Dutch Shell Corporation.[2] In the 1970s Pierce Wack's corporate planning team examined events that might impact the price of oil. They looked at what could cause the price of oil to change after years of stability in the market. They developed two scenarios for the company; one where the price of oil remained the same, and one where the price increased dramatically. The team presented their data and waited for managers to react. Nothing happened. The team then developed a new type of scenario. Instead of just looking at the data and trends, the group wrote stories to include the ramifications of the possible changes in the environment. These stories helped the managers imagine a very different future, and allowed managers to explore how they would react if the price of oil changed. As a consequence of the scenario development and subsequent analysis of the options available to the company, Royal Dutch Shell was one of the few companies to react quickly when the unthinkable happened: the 1973 oil crisis.

In this paper I will outline the technique of scenario planning and then provide the results of a mini-scenario-planning process we used at the University of Nebraska-Lincoln to look at collection development and digital information.

SCENARIO PLANNING STEPS

The practice of scenario development and planning can be broken down into eight basic steps.[3]

Step One: Identify the Focal Issue

In step one, the manager or planning team identifies the key question to be answered or considered in the process. The issue can be as broad as designing a mission statement and vision for an organization or as narrow as a single issue or question. Agreeing to the focus, though, is a key starting point. Unless the group understands the issue at hand, the group is unlikely to develop useful scenarios for the organization to consider.

Step Two: Key Factors in the Environment

Here the group lists the key factors in the environment that are relevant to the question at hand. This is the basic analysis of the environment that is a part of most planning processes and techniques and includes identifying strengths, weaknesses, opportunities and threats. The group should also identify economic, social, educational, technological, legal and political trends that affect the focal issue. In looking at collection development, key factors might include publishers' views of the future, budget considerations, inflation rates for library materials, or political changes that will impact what information is available and how that information is available.

Step Three: List the Driving Forces

In this step the group identifies those forces that will impact the future or are most likely to drive changes in the future. For example, in collection development, publisher pricing policies could be a driving force. Another driving force could be changes in user needs as the curriculum changes.

Step Four: Rank the Factors and Trends

Now the group ranks the factors or driving forces to pick out the most important forces and the most uncertain forces. These two elements–most important and most uncertain–will form the basis for the scenarios.

Step Five: Select the Plot Lines

The ranking exercise provides the axis for a matrix of possible plot lines. Each factor is placed on a continuum to yield four quadrants or four plot lines. The stories developed from these four options will move the group beyond best case, worst case thinking to considering alternatives that may be plausible in the changing environment.

Step Six: Write the Stories

Once the issues are identified and the directions of change outlined, the group can develop stories to describe possible futures. The plots need to be complete enough to capture a sense of the changes imagined by the group and simple enough to be usable. If the plots become too complex, decision makers may be lost in details that are not helpful in designing broad strategies. Each plot should have a name that captures the essence of the plot and helps decision makers relate to the story.

Step Seven: Develop the Implications

Once the stories are in place, the group can outline the implications of the stories. What does each story mean to the organization, to the governing body for the organization, to the front line decision maker? What strategies will be effective in coping with the environment if the scenario proves accurate? What contingencies can be put in place to ensure the greatest chance for the organization to survive? Which strategies are applicable to more than one scenario? How can the organization capitalize on this information to create its own future?

Step Eight: Selecting the Leading Indicators

Here the group outlines signposts to watch for to determine if the environment is moving in the direction of one scenario or another. Knowing what to watch for will provide feedback to managers as they decide which sets of strategies to implement as the environment changes. Signposts will help managers know which contingencies to implement, which options to choose, and when a strategy is likely to move the organization in a way that may decrease future flexibility if the manager guesses wrong on a developing trend.

WHEN SCENARIO PLANNING WORKS

Before embarking on a scenario planning process, managers should consider if the issue or concern is appropriate for a scenario-driven decision-making process. They need to carefully consider what types of uses lend themselves to scenario planning. Ideally, scenario planning works best when:

a. the external environment can evolve in fundamentally different ways. The outcome of these changes is not predetermined.
b. The organization cannot control change.
c. The change is permanent and structural.
d. The organization's actions are dependent upon the way the environment develops.
e. The organization cannot easily redo its decisions after the environment becomes clear.[4]

Scenario planning is a good technique, then, to help an organization address the issues that keep managers up at night.

HOW LONG SHOULD THE PROCESS TAKE

Scenario planning does require an investment in time by the participants. The entire process from identifying the initial question to be asked to outlining strategies that address the scenarios can take two to three months to complete. Participants need time between each step in the process to reflect on the information developed in the scenario sessions and to consider the implications of future actions.

DEVELOPING MINI-SCENARIOS

While the eight-step process for scenario-driven planning is very useful for leading a major planning effort, a simpler approach can be helpful when the problem for analysis is more focused or when time for planning is limited. For organizations that have completed a variety of planning processes and have available environment scans and other planning information, David Mercer suggests a simpler approach to scenario driven planning. Mercer outlines a six-step process for creating mini-scenarios. These steps are:

1. decide the drivers for change
2. bring drivers together into a viable framework
3. produce initial mini-scenarios
4. reduce to two to three scenarios
5. write the scenarios
6. identify the issues arising in the discussions[5]

The simpler approach encourages organizations with planning processes in place to build on the information already gathered in the organization and to use that information in designing scenarios of plausible futures.

For organizations that want to experiment with the process and need to engage participants in new dialogues about outstanding issues, mini-scenario planning sessions can be very effective. In one half-day session, a group that is knowledgeable about the issues and willing to entertain new ideas about the future can outline driving forces, identify key factors and create a matrix of plausible futures. The group can begin to develop the basic outlines of the mini-scenarios and assign someone to complete the story writing assignment. At a second session, the group can review the mini-scenarios and develop a preliminary set of strategies for each of the scenarios. Groups do need time between the two sessions to reflect on the scenarios. They also need time to thoroughly discuss options before outlining strategies and making decisions that could limit future actions of the organization.

POSSIBLE COLLECTION DEVELOPMENT SCENARIOS

At the University of Nebraska-Lincoln the Collection Development Committee used the simpler process outlined by David Mercer to develop four possible scenarios describing possible futures for collection development. The Committee began with the focused question: "How might the collection develop over the next five years?"

To answer that question the group first outlined the key factors or driving forces they saw impacting the libraries and collection development over the next five years. This yielded a list of over 25 items. The committee then grouped similar ideas to create a framework for analyzing change. The grouping of ideas helped the committee members identify overriding factors that could impact the collections in the future.

These groups of issues could yield a number of different and varied scenarios. The committee now had before them major themes that would be incorporated into the final scenarios.

For example, issues such as funding problems were taken as a given while issues predicting the inflation rate of serials were seen as less certain.

From the listing of themes, the group chose the two issues or factors that they saw as most important and most uncertain. The most important factor influencing development of the collection was the needs of the users. The most uncertain factor was the pricing policy of commercial publishers.

The committee developed a matrix based on these two forces (Figure 1). They divided user needs into undergraduate to graduate needs. They divided pricing strategies into monopolistic pricing and affordable pricing. From this matrix, the group identified four scenarios: the One Size Fits All (monopolistic pricing, undergraduate); the Virtual Undergraduate Library (affordable pricing, undergraduate); Researcher Heaven (graduate students, affordable); and Every Researcher on Their Own (monopolistic, graduate) (Figure 2).

The group discussed what they liked and disliked about each possible future as they explored the impact of these scenarios on the collection.

For example, in Every Researcher on Their Own, collection development changes from building collections to navigating the world of information to find non-local resources for researchers. This view of the future impacts many of the core values of collection development librarians in research libraries. The optimism of Researcher Heaven was a delightful contrast to both One Size Fits All and Every Researcher on Their Own. This world of affordable resources offered the collection development librarians the opportunity to look beyond traditional

FIGURE 1

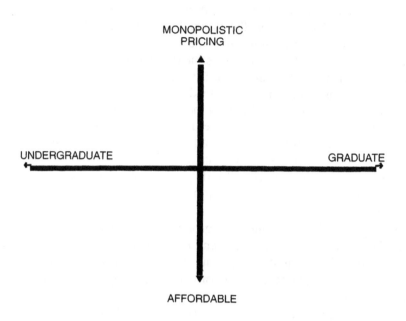

collection efforts to the creation and management of new knowledge. The scenario also raised the very real question of how to provide adequate support for the use of new technologies. The collection development librarians moved from thinking primarily about content to exploring the incorporation of new technologies into their plans.

The group identified strategies that might apply to these scenarios without trying to tie a strategy to a particular story. Strategies listed included: increasing document delivery, purchasing mostly print materials, purchasing mostly electronic material, scanning materials to produce digital archives, increasing hours of user support, purchasing a server for students to use to store their own research files, decreasing serial purchases, and decreasing monograph purchases. The group also looked at strategies to increase access to technology including increasing equipment and computer purchases, providing additional user help for solving computer problems, lobbying for funding for a wireless network, and working with vendors to develop user-friendly

FIGURE 2

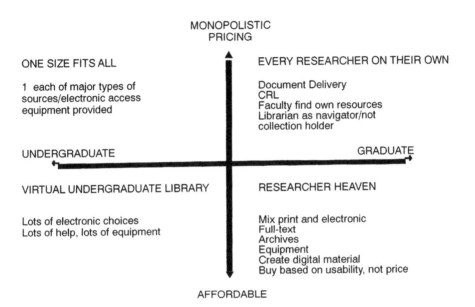

MONOPOLISTIC
PRICING

ONE SIZE FITS ALL | EVERY RESEARCHER ON THEIR OWN

1 each of major types of
sources/electronic access
equipment provided

Document Delivery
CRL
Faculty find own resources
Librarian as navigator/not
collection holder

UNDERGRADUATE | GRADUATE

VIRTUAL UNDERGRADUATE LIBRARY | RESEARCHER HEAVEN

Lots of electronic choices
Lots of help, lots of equipment

Mix print and electronic
Full-text
Archives
Equipment
Create digital material
Buy based on usability, not price

AFFORDABLE

interfaces to electronic products. These strategies address a variety of issues posed by the different scenarios.

The committee is now faced with prioritizing the options to identify those that fit the most number of scenarios. These options are the ones that the library can implement knowing that they will not hurt the library regardless of how the future develops. The committee must then examine those strategies that are more risky, i.e., those that apply to only 1 or 2 scenarios and decide if these strategies are worth the risks they represent.

In this simpler scenario planning process, the group chose to develop only two of the scenarios: the Virtual Undergraduate Library and One Size Fits All (see article Appendix). These scenarios brought life to the concepts the group had discussed and outlined the many issues the group needed to consider in prioritizing strategies.

CONCLUSION

What strategies should the library field outline to cope with these scenarios? Which current practices can survive if these futures become reality? Which strategies should we abandon if these scenarios reflect plausible futures?

These are the kinds of questions that face today's collection development librarian and today's managers. How can we prepare for an uncertain future? How can we develop contingencies that provide us with flexibility and keep future options open? We must have the courage to answer these questions, and the energy to explore them if we are to survive as viable institutions in a changing world.

Scenario planning then is not about predicting the future. It is not bound by today's world and it is not limited to thinking the unthinkable. Scenario planning is, however, a structured and disciplined technique that can be used to describe possible futures through carefully developed stories. The futures that are described in the stories are not mutually exclusive, they are not either/or types of plots. They are descriptions of plausible futures that can help managers cope with a variety of environmental changes that may impact their organizations.

NOTES

1. Council for Aid to Education, *Breaking the Social Contract: the Fiscal Crisis in Higher Education* (Santa Monica, CA: Rand Corporation, 1997): 22.

2. Joan Giesecke, *Scenario Planning for Libraries* (Chicago, IL: ALA editions, 1998), forthcoming.

3. Gordon Robbins, "Scenario Planning: A Strategic Alternative," Public Management, 77 (March, 1995): 7.

4. Wally Wood, "Where Do We Go From Here," *Across the Board*, 34 (March, 1997): 46.

5. David Mercer, "Simpler Scenarios," *Management Decisions*, 33 (July, 1995): 35.

APPENDIX

Scenario I-One Size Fits All

Chris and Pat, collection development librarians, were preparing information about the libraries' collections for new students. They were trying to present a positive picture for new students but faced a tough dilemma. They knew the library could afford to provide only a limited range of resources for students. Prices for library materials had become outrageous. Despite increases to the libraries' material budget, they were still unable to add to their limited collection.

Chris and Pat faced a world of monopolistic pricing. A few major firms controlled the publication and production of most of the standard electronic resources. Companies were charging for access to information on the Internet. The era of "free" information was long past.

The faculty had begun to realize the limitations of the libraries' collection and had lowered their expectation for what information students could access outside of the classroom. Nonetheless, students needed access to basic research sources to supplement classroom materials.

The Libraries' collection development policy was focused and limited. The Libraries aimed to serve the basic needs of the undergraduate population. The underlying collection development philosophy was that librarians hoped that one broad-based index or full-text service would cover most needed research. The librarians looked for that one key resource in each major area of the curriculum. The library subscribed to one electronic encyclopedia, one basic full-text journal data base and a few indexes. Other electronic resources became part of a fee-based service where students or faculty paid for access to specialized data bases. Limited print resources were available, although research items had to be obtained through interlibrary loan. Document delivery service was available on a cost recovery basis.

Chris and Pat tried to make the best of this situation. They emphasized that electronic resources were available on the campus network so that students could do much of their research from their dorms. They noted that the library had a leading-edge automated catalog and with links to a variety of resources. Ironically, the library had up-to-date public access work stations for student use as hardware prices had become quite reasonable. For a change, access to equipment was not an issue. Chris and Pat hoped that students would be willing to pay for access to research materials, but realized that most students limited themselves to the few subscriptions that were part of the network. Chris and Pat wondered if students even cared that student access to information resources was limited.

Scenario II–Virtual Undergraduate Library

Terry and Sam, collection development librarians, were quite pleased as they prepared materials about the libraries' collection for new students. The library was unveiling its new "Virtual Undergraduate Library Collection." The libraries now provided network access to a wide variety of electronic resources to support undergraduate student research. The publishing market for electronic resources had matured and competition had resulted in affordable products for undergraduate research. The libraries had been in a position to capitalize on these changes and had added a variety of resources to their core holdings. They now could boast of the wonderful global based catalog of indexes, full-text databases, and archival materials available to any member of the campus community.

Equipment issues had also been resolved. Hardware prices had continued to drop and the campus now boasted about its wireless network for students with computers, extensive computer labs, for those without computers, and adequate student help to guide students and faculty through the maze of electronic information available on campus.

Faculty were beginning to recognize how much the library had changed over time and were incorporating electronic resources into their teaching. The faculty knew they could demand more from the students because the library could and did provide access to more resources. Terry and Sam were pleased that they could help contribute to the education process by selecting and adding to the collection resources that could be used by the undergraduate population.

Role of the Aggregator
in the Emerging Electronic Environment

Kathleen Born

The traditional role of all players in the serials marketplace is un-settled with the advent of the electronic journal. Librarians, publishers, vendors are looking for ways to position themselves to take advantage of the new opportunities the emerging electronic environment prom-ises. Librarians look forward to the savings offered by easy access to journal articles. Publishers are trying various cost models for their new online versions. And vendors are exploring new initiatives to expand their role as an electronic intermediary. But like any uncharted territo-ry, there is an underlying sense of caution and risk attached to all players involved in coping with the electronic revolution. The trend toward embracing electronic journals affects librarians, publishers and vendors in different ways depending on their point of view. Based on their experience providing access to electronic journals, each player could argue one of the following statements:

THESIS A

The trend toward providing increased access to electronic journals presents a great opportunity for *Subscription Service Agents*, creates fear within *Publishers* and causes havoc for *Librarians*.

Kathleen Born is Vice President and Director of the Academic Division at EB-SCO Information Services in Birmingham, AL.

[Haworth co-indexing entry note]: "Role of the Aggregator in the Emerging Electronic Environment." Born, Kathleen. Co-published simultaneously in *Journal of Library Administration* (The Haworth Informa-tion Press, an imprint of The Haworth Press, Inc.) Vol. 28, No. 1, 1999, pp. 93-101; and: *Collection Development in a Digital Environment* (ed: Sul H. Lee) The Haworth Information Press, an imprint of The Haworth Press, Inc., 1999, pp. 93-101. Single or multiple copies of this article are available for a fee from The Haworth Document Delivery Service [1-800-342-9678, 9:00 a.m. - 5:00 p.m. (EST). E-mail address: getinfo@haworthpressinc.com].

THESIS B

The trend toward providing increased access to electronic journals presents a great opportunity for *Publishers*, creates fear within *Librarians*, and causes havoc for *Subscription Service Agents*.

THESIS C

The trend toward providing increased access to electronic journals presents a great opportunity for *Librarians*, creates fear within *Subscription Agents*, and causes havoc for *Publishers*.

TRADITIONAL ROLE

The familiar relationship between the library, publisher and agent continues to exist as libraries place orders for print and electronic journals with the agent. Agents provide the payment to publishers, consolidate customer billing and handle servicing the orders with personal representatives, automation interfaces and management reports. Publishers continue to disseminate scholarly information through the print journal and are producing their journals electronically. Consequently, agents are experiencing a rapid growth of electronic title records in their databases. Librarians forced to cancel print subscriptions due to escalating prices are hopeful that the electronic journal will be a more cost-effective alternative to the paper subscription.

NEW ROLE

As a result of the e-journal coming of age the traditional relationship between the library, the publisher and the agent has changed. The existing functions between the three players continue for print subscriptions but in the electronic arena, the agent must make major modifications to their service to remain a viable player in the next decade.

A new model is unfolding. The subscription agent assumes a new role as an electronic intermediary and the new name of aggregator. As an aggregator, the subscription agent acts as an intermediary who assembles, or aggregates, the electronic journals from multiple publishers and offers the end user access to the library's electronic journals through a single location. Powerful search engines manipulated through a Web browser enable users to access and order Web-based journals via the Internet.

CUSTOMER EXPECTATIONS

Prior to developing a new service, the agent must listen to customers, see a need and fill the gap. Seminars, meetings and discussion groups are venues to ensure the user and administrative requirements are incorporated into the design of the service.

Foremost on the list of customer input is the desire to have a single site and a common interface to access all electronic journals in the library collection. The authentication process should be simplified to eliminate the need for user names and passwords but flexible enough to allow authentication methods from multiple locations.

The user wants the ability to search across the content of all publishers in the collection with links to the full text on the aggregator's server or the publisher's server. Customers desire links to full text from the library's online public access catalog, from subject databases and from a table of contents service.

Standard full text periodical databases suitable for undergraduate academic libraries are offered by several database providers. As more of a library's core titles are published electronically, database providers are asked to customize an electronic journal package to match the library's core collection. Other libraries prefer to work with an agent to unbundle the e-journal packages to permit selection of individual journal subscriptions. Usage statistics by title and database, collection management reports and archiving journal back files for perpetual access remain high on the list of customer expectations from the agent's new electronic journal service. If license agreements follow a standardized model, many librarians prefer the agent handle the licensing process with the publisher.

WORKING ARRANGEMENTS WITH PUBLISHERS

The long-established business relationships between subscription agents and publishers has facilitated the extension of the working arrangements into the age of the electronic journal. In the print environment a gentleman's handshake sealed the working relationship between publisher and agent; however, in the electronic age, a signed agreement confirms the operating methods for both parties. An agent's agreement with an online publisher specifies whether the journal content will reside on the agent's server or on the publisher's server; the file format of the data; and the agent's schedule to import the publisher's files. Part of the technical handshake between publisher and agent includes procedures for user authentication and assurances the data is distributed securely. The working agreement reflects the publisher's approach to electronic distribution. While some publishers allow any user to search, browse and view all abstracts and tables of contents others grant access rights to subscribers only.

Publishers provide journal content in various formats thus requiring an electronic journal delivery system to be flexible in order to accommodate the diversified file formats from publishers. Claiming and routine technical support will be available through agents. In anticipation of opening new distribution channels, publishers are asking agents for assistance in marketing their electronic offerings to users outside their normal subscription base.

PRICING MODELS

Publishers are experimenting with various pricing models for online journals as evidenced by searching a subscription agent's database. For example, EBSCO's database has 2,700 primary listings for online journals. More than half are free with the print subscription. For other print/online combinations, it costs ten to twenty percent more. Some of the larger online journal packages are priced the same as the print with an added percentage. Only a small number of publishers offer a discount for the online journal without the print counterpart. Publishers will ultimately settle on an electronic pricing model which maintains the current revenue stream.

THE AGENT'S RESPONSE

Subscription agents realize the traditional role of the vendor must coexist with the emerging parallel reality of serving libraries in the electronic age. At first glance the emerging role of the agency is blurry and hard to define. Many new players, such as commercial publishers and non-profit organizations, are positioning themselves to serve as aggregators of electronic journals. Subscription agencies are in a unique position to design an online journal delivery service due to their knowledge of the library's serials collections, the long-standing relationships with librarians and publishers and the existing technical support infrastructure. They are developing new dynamic models for loading or pointing to the journal content and managing access to electronic journals.

All models constructed by subscription agents will facilitate ordering, access and management of electronic journals from a single source. To accomplish this goal, agents are forming partnerships with publishers, database providers, table of contents services, and commercial document delivery suppliers. Users will navigate through these integrated services using a single search engine to access the aggregator's server. (See Figure 1.)

FIGURE 1

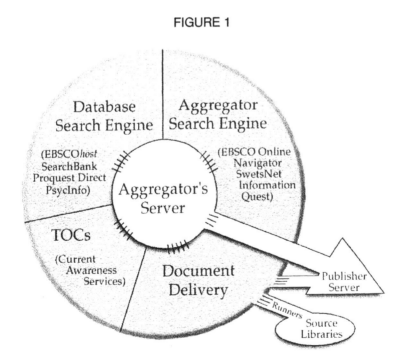

AGGREGATOR'S SERVER

The new service model centers around the aggregator's server which contains information about the library's or end user's subscriptions and services ordered through the agent. The server controls the "gates" to each component of the model allowing a search to pass to the appropriate service to retrieve the information. It will read the customer file and determine which services a user has rights to access to complete the search.

The goal of the searcher is to retrieve the full text of an article. The request or inquiry can be executed from any entry point on the model, for example, through a subject database, the electronic journal collection, a document delivery supplier or through a table of contents or current awareness service. The system's software will integrate these services from a single entry point passing the request through the authorized information service channels to arrive at the full text of an article.

CURRENT AGGREGATOR SERVICES

At this time the components of the model operate independently. A customer can access their electronic journals through an aggregator's gateway to conduct a search. Using the interface provided by the Web-based search engine, the user can browse all titles on the system or conduct a search by author, article title, journal title, keyword or by subject. Access to electronic journals is authenticated through the agents' record of the library's subscription order or authenticated directly by the publisher. A user can view all volumes, issues and years covered by the subscription to the electronic journal. The results list displays an icon if the full text can be viewed on the aggregator's server. If not, the user is linked to the publishers' server to view the full text of the article.

Presently most agents offer a Web-based commercial document delivery service as a stand-alone service. The process begins with a user entering a citation, the supplier's search engine scans their database to locate the best source to retrieve the article. Some requests are filled electronically where transactional rights are in place. The majority of requests are routed to a source library where the document is scanned or photocopied and delivered by Ariel, facsimile, mail or courier. Most libraries will block local holdings to prevent ordering a document which is housed in their local collection. Consortia members check the request against the holdings of member libraries before fulfilling through a commercial document supplier.

INTEGRATED SERVICES

Periodical Full Text Databases

A general reference or subject specific full text database may be the access point for a student or faculty member seeking information on a topic. The user conducts a search within the database, locates the full text article and prints or downloads the article to complete the session.

The new search engine will continue the search if the full text is not available in the periodical database. Future enhancements will link the citation to the user's electronic subscriptions to search for the article. If the electronic text is not on subscription, the citation is linked to the document delivery service where traditional methods are used to obtain the article from the publisher or photocopied from a source library.

Electronic Journal Delivery System

Authorized users can browse, search, view, print or download the full text of an article from a journal on subscription through the agents' electronic journal delivery system. They can view abstracts and the tables of contents of all titles in the e-journal system. When the desired full text is not on subscription, forthcoming enhancements will link the request to the full text databases authorized by the customer profile. Ultimately if the full text is not located, the request is passed to the document delivery option for fulfillment.

Document Delivery

Library policy may allow certain users such as faculty or graduate students to use the document delivery service without mediation by the interlibrary loan staff. In the future once the citation is input into the document delivery component, the system will search for the article in the authorized full text databases and electronic journal subscriptions. If the article is located it is delivered to the requester. If not, the request follows the normal document delivery channels to locate the article and deliver it to the end user.

Table of Contents

Users subscribing to a table of contents service can take advantage of push technology and receive relevant information in a timely fashion with minimal effort. When the TOC is ready, the server delivers or pushes it automatically to the user's computer. If a citation is selected, the aggregator's system links to the full text databases and electronic journals on subscription. If the full text is not present and rights exist for ordering documents, the document delivery avenue is opened to fulfill the request.

OPAC and Web Sites

Aggregators will provide gateways outside of their services to connect the user to full text information. Accessing the library's Web site may be the easiest way for a user to browse the electronic journal collection. Or the user may prefer to link from the Web-based Online Public Access Catalog (OPAC) using a link from the 856 field of the MARC record to reach the full text through the aggregator's service. Aggregators will provide the necessary links to help the user navigate to the electronic full text of an institution's subscriptions. The integration of services will be accomplished through strategic partnerships between the agent and the provider or by linking separate services within the divisions of an information provider.

MANAGEMENT OF ELECTRONIC RESOURCES

Collection managers are involved in the management of electronic resources in their library. It is often difficult to determine which periodical full text databases and online journals are accessed most often or which print subscriptions have an online version. Database producers assist by providing management reports and statistical information on title, database and session usage of periodical full text databases. The usage reports are instrumental in helping collection managers make decisions concerning present and future electronic purchases.

Reports from subscription agents identify the electronic journals on order, the format and the delivery method. A list of the library's print subscriptions available in an electronic format can be requested by collection managers interested in switching from print subscriptions to online access. With the integration of services, aggregators will provide combined reports showing the library's print subscriptions, electronic journals, periodical full text databases and document purchases. Comprehensive reporting of expenditures on journals and individual articles will be a major benefit for collection development and budgetary planning.

CONCLUSION

Subscription agents will continue to develop their electronic journal delivery models based on the expectations of the users. To remain a participant in the information industry, agents will remain open to changing traditional methods and approaches to service. The electronic revolution is in its early stages. It is an expensive venture to remain a player in the information industry. It requires taking risks and making investments in technology, staff and customer support as part of a long-term commitment.

Technology is driving change. We are exploring new territory with technological advances enabling us to pioneer new ways of doing business. Flexibility is the key to long-term success. Agents have to keep the needs and expectations of the user clearly in focus as we plan our strategies for the future. The solutions will differ among agents and other players in the information industry depending on the culture of each organization. The philosophy of the company's leadership will affect the way each business approaches their solution and how quickly they respond to change. It will be up to the library and end user to examine the choices and decide which model works best in their environment.

Digital Information
and the Subscription Agent
as Information Coach

Kit Kennedy

The affinity between the mission of the library community and the work of Matisse amazes and reassures me. Where Matisse revolutionized tradition reusing the common object within a new partnership of color and shape, library communities are rethinking, revisiting, and albeit sometimes re-worrying the common issues. Yet, it is in this reworking of common concerns where training and coaching increasingly play a role in the suggestion of solution that makes this community such a vibrant landscape.

Libraries are simply miraculous.

Of the goo-gobs of marvelous things that libraries do, I am amazed and once again reassured that they are seedbeds for some of the most compelling mission statements every crafted. Five such examples leap to mind:

1. Books are for use.
2. Every book its reader.
3. Every reader his book.
4. Save the time of the reader.
5. The library is a growing organism.[1]

Kit Kennedy is Director of Academic Sales at Blackwell's Information Services in San Francisco, CA.

[Haworth co-indexing entry note]: "Digital Information and the Subscription Agent as Information Coach." Kennedy, Kit. Co-published simultaneously in *Journal of Library Administration* (The Haworth Information Press, an imprint of The Haworth Press, Inc.) Vol. 28, No. 1, 1999, pp. 103-112; and: *Collection Development in a Digital Environment* (ed: Sul H. Lee) The Haworth Information Press, an imprint of The Haworth Press, Inc., 1999, pp. 103-112. Single or multiple copies of this article are available for a fee from The Haworth Document Delivery Service [1-800-342-9678, 9:00 a.m. - 5:00 p.m. (EST). E-mail address: getinfo@haworthpressinc.com].

103

Let me continue this Prologue by sharing a few definitions and several observations before getting to the central topic: how in a digitized environment the vendor's role is expanding to encompass a more active coaching component.

DEFINITIONS

Definitions are curious organisms–signposts really. They don't tell you where you need to go, but they can map a way for you to get where you think you're planning to be. That we try to define things matters; that we are willing to revisit our definitions matters more.

How I define libraries seems to expand yearly to embrace the new and hybrid players: libraries (real and virtual), librarians, consortiums (both formal and informal, a.k.a. self-defining), publishers (commercial, societal, Internet, Webpagers), corporations, vendors, aggregators, and readers. My professional experience is primarily with academic and research librarians so my comments are heavily weighted in their arena. While the word "vendor" encompasses all middle-added-service-providers, in this paper I am referring to subscription agents who provide core services as well as serve as information providers and aggregators.

Why didn't I include the end-user? To use a library one must read: be a reader. In my mind, the reader is synonymous with the library patron, library user, and the end-user. Of course, readers have options. They can use other forms of "libraries" such as bookstores and Internet not provided through the library. Besides, the word "reader" has a nobility of spirit and purpose that "end-user" cannot muster. Reading and learning are not the end of all use.

Finally, the digital environment grapples with digitized information. Let us move on to 4 observations.

OBSERVATIONS

1. The centrality of the reader is paramount.
2. There is no escaping tradition, time, and the future.
3. Our professional environment is akin to white water rafting.
4. The expectations for librarians are changing.

CENTRALITY OF THE READER

See also definitions above. Readers are made not born. They receive "coaching" on how and even what not to read. Readers read regardless of format, location or delivery method of format. What they want to read (be it a perceived or a real need), they want available to them immediately. Readers read in real time.

NO ESCAPING TRADITION, TIME AND THE FUTURE

Tradition is what we now do in the present. Time, unfortunately for many of us, is the quick two-step breath between deadlines, and the future is what we do in our next breath. The compression of our activities and the ramification of this evolution are staggering. As a Disney Fellow Danny Hillis states, "The first steps in the story of evolution took a billion years. The next step–nervous systems and brains–took a few hundred million years. The next steps, including the development of language, took less than a million years. And the most recent steps seem to be taking only a few decades. The process is feeding on itself and becoming autocatalytic."[2]

WE MIGHT ALL BE PARTICIPANTS IN WHITE WATER RAFTING

Personally, I have resisted the image of our professional life as one of change as in white water rafting. But I can no longer deny this metaphor although I will suggest later, if not an ending, at least the hope of calming interludes. There are lessons to be shared in surviving this experiential change. And I do stress the surviving of stress. Nevertheless, I imagine white water rafting offers the following: there is purpose to this activity. You get somewhere, hopefully, to an end. You deal with change. Your survival is often dependent upon quick thinking and action. You are not spending your waking and sleeping hours writing memos, strategic plans, nor core competencies. You are not acting as an island. The physical environment matters. You are not disassociated from your body. You feel good, fulfilled and/or energized. Possibly, you feel grateful. You can and will talk about it. Your time has been well spent; you will make a place for it in your life. You have been smitten by leisure activity.

Now, for that promised calming interlude. I suggest white water rafting does begin and end. At the endings, you can sit down, pick up an article on this sport. In short, you read. Also in a perverse way I might add, there are probably no Internet connections in this kind of rafting, nor are cell phones or pagers viable options.

PROFESSIONAL EXPECTATIONS FOR LIBRARIANS ARE INCREASING

Economic pressures, subsequent reorganization and tweaking if not raising of the infrastructure, as well as the complexity, high visibility and the price-ticket of information, play topsy-turvy with the professional expectations, not to mention job longevity, for librarians. Recent job postings on Internet calling for disparate skills and training make this "writing on the wall." It is not fantasy to image the following "opportunity": Senior level position in library, 1 year contract renewable every three months. Person needs to demonstrate the following core competencies: white water rafting, customer service, collection development for leisure science in the millennium, microbiology, and information science. Must be Internet-savvy; demonstrate working knowledge of networks and networking (hardware, software, virtual ware, and consortium); expertise in licensing. Sits on Provost's council for digitized projects; liaisons with distance learning coordinators. Liaisons with the end-users group. Requires proven negotiation skills. Fund raising a plus. An advertising and/or marketing background will be considered. A sense of humor, while not required, will be taken into consideration. Publishers need not apply.

This exaggerating, tongue-and-cheek description is not to bemoan or belittle academe nor corporations, but to call attention to the pressures on librarians.

Now that we have looked at several definitions and observations, we are ready to move into the central topic: VENDOR AS IC.

DIGITIZED INFORMATION REQUIRES THE VENDOR TO BECOME AN IC (INFORMATION COACH)

Let us take a brief look at how the role of vendors is changing in the digitized environment. We will listen to both a librarian and vendor.

Jim Mouw, head of serials at University of Chicago, suggests under a new model three shifts: vendors will launch new products, there will be a blending of titles and indexing, and vendors will manage both the subscription and the access.[3] Clearly, we are quickly moving from the either-or situation of ownership versus access, into the realm of ownership and access.

Suzanne Wilson Higgins of Blackwell's Information Services raises interesting issues about the vendor supplying a "virtual pie." For instance, she asks the difficult, "How does a vendor provide infrastructure for transferring digital objects between parties?" She states the "supply and availability of hi-tech products varies greatly from market to market, as standards emerge and a true market emerges."[4]

Further, she summarizes with digitized information, vendors provide:

- electronic service
- electronic acquisitions administration
- electronic budgetary control
- advice and support for electronic publications
- assistance with electronic access
  electronic marketing and usage information
- arbitrating and documenting agreed terms.[5]

This is what vendors have always done: supplying and managing traditional core services but now with a digital spin.

The author concludes, "A new generation of middlemen is needed."[6] I suggest that digitized information is the shaper of how vendors are expanding their roles. In addition to providing core subscription services, vendors are in the business and technology as aggregators and information coaches.

QUALITIES OF COACHING

First, a caveat. While the digitized environment increases contact between vendor and publisher seven-fold, this paper limits itself to the coaching experiences between vendor and library. Second, another caveat. For my examples and terminology, I have refrained from drawing on athletics as a source of metaphor for coaching although there are compelling similarities.

Let us take a few minutes to look at coaching in general. Coaching can be formal and informal. It can be as structured as a training course. It can be as informal and brief as an impromptu telephone conversation or e-mail exchange between colleagues to help answer a question. Informal coaching welcomes walk-ins. Coaching displays a low-tolerance for whining. Mentoring is a subset of coaching. One can be mentored, one can be coached through programs, by individuals, by books, and through hands-on experience and tutorials. Age and time, especially "free" time, might be our most precious mentors.

Coaching is no stranger to libraries. Libraries have traditionally invested in the coaching function as part of its core mission. Examples include bibliographic instruction, the reference interview, computer labs (hardware and software), Internet training, and disseminating information on research and study skills.

WHY DO VENDORS INVEST IN COACHING?

The one-word answer is longevity. The longer answer is: coaching crystallizes the problem, removes the stumbling blocks, suggests a solution, supports a creative framework for thinking, empowers and energizes the staff it doesn't scare off, and identifies hidden opportunities. Vendors who succeed over time will be those who manage both sides of coaching: external and intra-company coaching. While information coaching can be an expensive time-guzzler with providing sometimes delayed results, it is a critical investment for survival.

EXTERNAL COACHING

In the digitized environment, vendors help coach libraries in the following:

- bibliography information and advice
- licensing
- networking
- product/service awareness
- industry/market advice

Vendors serve as sounding-boards for libraries. Vendors have traditionally provided training and coaching for their propriety software and products, but the digitized environment has increased the scope and depth of what's needed and expected. The wick has been turned up. Librarians who have experienced first-hand the frustration of tracking down an Internet publication for a faculty member and then attempting to establish an order, now look toward their "traditional" vendor to provide the same service for digitized information as those vendors do for print format. Many librarians have said to me, "I expect my vendor to get serial publications for my library–no matter what format, no matter from whom or what. I expect you to know from whom to get it, to fix it when it no longer comes or is defective, and advise me of the cost implications."

A further comment on advice. Libraries seek vendors to advise or coach them on the practical (ordering of digitized information), the people-networking aspect (advising them what other libraries are doing or not doing), into the realm of crystal-balling the future (what will it cost our library). Vendors are frequently asked to reassure the library of the vendor's solvency and technological commitment. The question is usually phrased, "How is your company gearing up, managing, responding to library requirements to handle digitized information?" We expect to see such questions included on RFPs and RFIs.

The bibliographic inquiries for digitized information place an interesting and new spin on the complexity that was once dominated by combinations and membership packages (those problematic parent/child relationships). Vendors are also gearing up to provide new titles altering services for digitized information.

Libraries look for vendors to assist them in advising on licensing and/or providing links for additional information. Vendors, like libraries, are fundamentally committed to standards, are working toward simplifying, streamlining, and standardizing licensing whenever possible. The operative is "moving towards" as opposed to a fixed reality.

Frequently libraries want to know what other libraries and/or consortiums are doing with digital information. The question is often asked, "Who else is signed up with you?" Sometimes the question comes with a slight twist, "I understand that such-and-such a vendor can provide this service. What does your company offer?"

Because the relationship between libraries and vendors has been both a business as well as a collegial one, libraries rely on vendors to be synthesizers (eyes and ears) of the market and industry. Libraries frequently ask advice on what implications (including cost) for shifting a portion of their collection from print to digitized access. Recently, a library director asked me about my company's thoughts on owning versus leasing of equipment.

Vendors have a long-standing tradition of alerting libraries of what is new in the market by demoing and providing training/coaching opportunities of their new products and services. Vendors create venues for coaching and education through technology showcases, participating in professional organizations, conferences and through disseminating information on their Websites, as well as onsite visits from company representatives.

Let us move into the second and last part of vendor coaching.

INTRA-COMPANY COACHING

I choose the word "intra-company" making the similar distinction as does Internet and Intranet. I shy away from the term inter-company coaching because that seems to denote vendors coaching each other. Of course, vendors do learn from each other–often quickly and sometimes very painfully. In addition, vendors do coach each other publicly and constructively when they mutually participate in standards work. Coaching is never in a vacuum. Coaching is a participatory sport.

As is with libraries, so it is with vendors: coaching is both formal and informal. Increasingly vendors are creatively applying resources to establish an infrastructure to supply programs and opportunities for intra-company coaching. New positions for coach-trainers assist staff in keeping current with new and/or revised software, new products and services, digital information, and increased demands from customers for advice/support. All of these new opportunities must be met while maintaining quality service levels. These coach-trainer positions also provide career paths for staff. Human Resource Departments within vendors are tailoring coaching programs in tandem with outside consultants and off-site training companies. Expert partners are developed within organizations for specialized functions. Vendors set up specialized teams to manage the requirements of customers and help coach staff. Expert partners are circles of knowing and when informal are self-regulating. They live as long as they have a purpose. Your expertise is only what you are willing to share or network with a coaching attitude. "We've always done it that way," is no longer part of the fabric.

Because vendors support both onsite and remote staff, they face unique challenges, similar to those of libraries with distance learning programs and/or branch campuses. Remote employees learn to coach each other often through e-mail, advising colleagues of a solution to a situation that might otherwise turn into a problem for the many. Coaching is by nature pro-active problem-solving. Remote users live in an immediacy of coaching. They are practical, expedient, fluid, and non-hierarchical in their coaching requirements. It often comes down to this "who knows" question, "Who do I know who knows what I need to know to fix this problem and can I reach them immediately?"

With the complexity of what needs to get done, one of the challenges for vendors is to coach staff on who does what. In other words, who to go to for help. The traditional organizational chart with the subsequent telephone or e-mail directory no longer cuts it. With the complexity as a byproduct of the digitized environment, vendors work to maintain and communicate clear and straightforward contacts for customers and staff.

To keep staff informed and up-to-speed, vendors are establishing an Intranet so staff can download demos, pick up press releases in advance of publication and distribution, and keep current on sales and marketing information including product information.

TWO CONCLUDING COMMENTS

As we coach, so we are coached. Let us remember the comment of Laurie Anderson, "Technology is the campfire around which we tell our stories."[7]

So, where does this leave us? In other words, where do we begin? "The world remains weird . . . weird and luminal. . . . Get used to it, and revel."[8]

NOTES

1. S. R. Ranganathan's FIVE LAWS OF LIBRARY SCIENCE. For further discussion of these laws see Crawford, Walt and Michael Gorman. FUTURE LIBRARIES: Dreams, Madness & Reality. Chicago and London: American Library Association, 1995, p. 7-8. For further discussion of Ranganathan's "new laws" see Gorman, Michael. OUR SINGULAR STRENGTH: Meditations for Librarians. Chicago and London: American Library Association, 1998, p. 61-69.

2. Hillis, Danny, "The Big Picture," WIRED 6.01 (January 1998), p. 38.

3. Mouw, James. Presentation at the 1997 NASIC Conference (Changing Roles–the Library Perspective), publication pending.

4. Wison Higgins, Suzanne, "Simple Simon's Experience of Buying a Virtual Pie: The Pieman's Perspective," SERIALS, Vol 10 no 3 (November 1997), p. 303.

5. Ibid., p. 302.

6. Ibid., p. 302.

7. Anderson, Laurie, "State of the Planet 1998," WIRED 6.01 (January 1998), pp. 202-203.

8. Gilder, George, "Happy Birthday Wired," WIRED 6.01 (January 1998), pp. 40, 42.

Index

AAU, *See* Association of American
    Universities (AAU)
Academic libraries
    changing roles of, 3-6,13-16,20-24,
        56-59,81-82
    defining, 104
    disintermediation, 35,56-60
    traditional models of, 23-24
Academic server model of scholarly
    publishing, 15-16
Access to information, *See*
    Information access
ACLS, *See* American Council of
    Learned Societies (ACLS)
Advantages of
    digital libraries, 9-10
    electronic publishing, 10-11
    print publishing, 10
    scenario planning, 81-83
Africana Librarians Council of the
    African Studies Association
    (ALC/ASA), 75
Agents (subscription), *See*
    Subscription agents
Aggregator model of subscription
    agents, 93-101
Agreements (licensing), *See* Licensing
    and copyright issues
AIP, *See* American Institute of Physics
    (AIP)
ALA, *See* American Library
    Association (ALA)
ALC/ASA, *See* Africana Librarians
    Council of the African Studies
    Association (ALC/ASA)
American Council of Learned
    Societies (ACLS), 75-77
American Institute of Physics (AIP)
    and professional ethics
    issues, 34,36-40

American Library Association (ALA),
    Statement of Professional
    Ethics, 35
American Physical Society (APS) and
    professional ethics issues, 34,
    36-40
Anderson, L., 111
APS, *See* American Physical Society
    (APS)
Area studies collections, 63-80
ARL, *See* Association of Research
    Libraries (ARL)
Association of American Universities
    (AAU), Taskforce on the
    Acquisition and Distribution
    of Foreign and Area Studies
    Materials, 64-65
Association of Research Libraries
    (ARL), 15-16,26,64-65,68f,70

Bailey, C.W., 25,27
Baker, N., 20
Barschall, H., 34,36-40
Berra, Y., 4
Bible (Old Testament, Book of
    Daniel), 50
Blackwell's Information Services
    (subscription agent), 103-112
Books
    Electronic books, *See* Electronic
        publishing
    Printed books, *See* Print publishing
Born, K., 2,93
Bourdieu, P., 20
Budgetary issues, 7,14-15,19,23-24,
    25-26,64,66-70. *See also*
    Downsizing collections. *See
    also* Pricing issues

Perrault, A., 69
Pew Higher Education Roundtable, 14
Physical infrastructure issues, *See*
    Infrastructure issues
Planning (scenario), *See* Scenario
    planning
Plato, 49
Pricing issues, 24-27,64-70,87-89,96
Print publishing
    advantages of, 10
    impact of culture on, 49-52
    impact of Internet publishing on,
        56-57
Privacy issues, 12-13. *See also*
    Licensing and copyright
    issues
Professional ethics issues
American Library Association (ALA),
    Statement on Professional
    Ethics, 35
    background information on, 33-34
    disintermediation, 35
    Elsevier Pergamon
        (publishers)/MIT press
        (publishers) and *History of*
        European Ideas/European
        Legacy, 34,40-42
    Gordon & Breach (publisher)
        litigation against Barschall,
        the American Institute of
        Physics, and the American
        Physical Society, 34,36-40
    librarian responsibilities, 44-46
    licensing and copyright issues, 11,
        24-26,33-34,40-45,63-64,95,
        108-110
    relevance of, 35
Publications costs, *See* Pricing issues
Publishers (roles of), 22-23,47-50,
    93-101,103-112
Publishing
    electronic, *See* Electronic
        publishing
    Internet *See* Internet publishing
    print, *See* Print publishing
    scholarly, *See* Scholarly publishing

Qualities of information coaches,
    107-108

Rand Corporation (Council to Aid
    Education), 81
Ranganathan, S.R., 103
Relationship between libraries,
    publishers, and subscription
    agents, 47-48,94-95,103-112
Research Libraries Group (RLG), 75-76
Research publishing, *See* Scholarly
    publishing
Resource sharing issues 7,15,24,
    26-27,43-44,63-80. *See also*
    Cooperative collection
    development. *See also*
    Interlibrary loan (ILL)
Right to information access, 44-47
RLG, *See* Research Libraries Group
    (RLG)
Roles of
    academic libraries, 3-6,13-16,
        20-23,57-59,81-82
    publishers, 22-23,47-50,93-101,
        103-112
    subscription agents, 22-23,47-50,
        93-101,103-112
Rosenblum, W., 24
Rosetto, L., 48
Royal Dutch Shell Corporation, 82
Runkle, M. 29
Rushdie, S. 17

SALALM, *See* Seminar on the
    Acquisition of Latin
    American Library Materials
    (SALALM)
Scenario planning
    background, 81-83
    collection-need/user-need matrices,
        88f,89f
    examples of, 86-91
    length of process, 85-86
    scenario planning steps, 83-85
    when to implement, 85

T - #0202 - 101024 - C0 - 229/152/7 [9] - CB - 9780789007940 - Gloss Lamination